MOBILITIES, NETWORKS, GEOGRAPHIES

Mobilities, Networks, Geographies

JONAS LARSEN
Roskilde University, Denmark

JOHN URRY
Lancaster University, UK

KAY AXHAUSEN
Eidgenoessische Technische Hochschule (ETH), Switzerland

ASHGATE

Published by
Ashgate Publishing Limited
Gower House
Croft Road
Aldershot
Hampshire GU11 3HR
England

Ashgate Publishing Company
Suite 420
101 Cherry Street
Burlington, VT 05401-4405
USA

Ashgate website: http://www.ashgate.com

British Library Cataloguing in Publication Data
Larsen, Jonas
   Mobilities, networks, geographies. - (Transport and society)
   1.Transportation - Social aspects 2.Social networks
   3.Communication - Social aspects
   I.Title II.Urry, John III.Axhausen, K. W., 1958-
   303.4'832

Library of Congress Cataloging-in-Publication Data
Larsen, Jonas.
   Mobilities, networks, geographies / by Jonas Larsen, John Urry, and Kay Axhausen.
       p. cm. -- (Transport and society)
   Includes bibliographical references and index.
   ISBN-13: 978-0-7546-4882-6
   ISBN-10: 0-7546-4882-6
   1. Transportation. 2. Social networks. 3. Population geography. I. Urry, John.
II. Axhausen, K. W., 1958- III. Title.

   HE148.L37 2006
   303.48'32--dc22

   2006018478

ISBN-13: 978-0-7546-4882-6
ISBN-10: 0 7546 4882 6

Printed and bound in Great Britain by MPG Books Ltd. Bodmin, Cornwall.

Contents

List of Figures, Maps and Tables

Figures

Maps – Separate Plate Section Between Pages 88 and 89

Tables

Preface

This book is a substantially revised version of the report 'Social Networks and Future Mobilities' commissioned by the UK Department for Transport (DfT), produced between October 2004 and October 2005, and submitted early 2006. We are very grateful for this financial support but the views expressed in this book are ours; DfT is not responsible for the material or arguments presented here. Kay Axhausen, ETH, Switzerland and John Urry, Lancaster, UK were the principal investigators on this project. Jonas Larsen was the research fellow based in the Centre for Mobilities Research within the Sociology Department at Lancaster University. Jonas Larsen is now based at Roskilde University in Denmark.

We would very much like to thank the steering committee of this project for their very helpful comments and advice: Steve Atkins, Margaret Grieco, Ian Hawthorne and Peter Jones. We are especially grateful to Margaret Grieco, who commissioned this book as part of her Ashgate series on Transport and Society. We also thank the 24 youngish people that we interviewed in the beginning of 2005. They provided illuminating accounts of their social networks and travel and communication practices, and this book is very much a product of these interviews.

We are also indebted to the invaluable comments and support we received at a workshop held in the Institute for Advanced Studies at Lancaster University in December 2005 where we presented the DfT report and received excellent feedback.

We are very grateful, too, to Timo Ohnmacht and Andreas Frei, ETH, Switzerland, who provided much technical and computing support for this research both at-a-distance and during the period Timo spent as an intern at Lancaster University.

Other 'mobilities' colleagues that assisted this project include Jørgen Ole Bærenholdt, Javier Caletrio, Noel Cass, Tim Edensor, Michael Haldrup, Kevin Hannam, Juliet Jain, Vincent Kaufmann, Eric Laurier, Christian Licoppe, Glenn Lyons, Dean MacCannell, Jennie Germann Molz, Mimi Sheller, Elizabeth Shove, Laura Watts and Barry Wellman.

Jonas Larsen would like to express his gratitude to Will Medd, Jennie Germann Molz and John Urry for being exceptionally good colleagues at Lancaster University. But most importantly, he would like to thank his partner Johanna for her tremendous support when she moved to the UK so soon after giving birth to their son Elliot, who is certainly born into a mobile world.

And many thanks to Pennie Drinkall and Claire O'Donnell who provided exceptional administrative support for the project within CeMoRe and the Sociology Department at Lancaster University.

Chapter 1

Researching Networks and Travel: An Introduction

Introduction: Mobile Societies

'Time–space compression' is said to characterize modern societies (Harvey 1989). And yet there appear to be significant further changes taking place as to how social life is distributed over time, over space and over people's life-course. 'Time–space compression' also seems to involve time–space distanciation, that is the geographical spreading of people's social networks. The last decade or two has seen striking increases in travel and in longer-distance communications through mobile phone calls, text messaging and email. 'Ordinary' people in prosperous societies are increasingly on the move *and* communicating more to connect with absent others. There seems to be a shift from 'little boxes' of spatially dense and socially overlapping networks to *networks* where connections are spatially dispersed and membership of one network does not necessarily overlap with that of others (Castells 1996, 2000; Wellman 2002; Urry 2003; Axhausen 2005a, 2005b). Thus as the easy availability of cars, trains, planes and communication technologies seem to spread social networks beyond cities, regions and nations, so they reconnect people by helping to afford intermittent visits, meetings and frequent communication at-a-distance. People can travel, relocate and migrate and yet still be connected with friends and family members 'back home' and elsewhere. So, increasingly, people who are near 'emotionally' may be 'geographically' far apart; yet they are only a journey, email or a phone call away. Thus developments in transport and communication technologies not merely service or connect people but appear to reconfigure social networks by both disconnecting *and* reconnecting them in complex ways.

This book will show how contemporary technologies and practices of transport and communication are reconfiguring how people connect with places and each other, how they socialize with and relate to friends, workmates and family members, and how they make new contacts often at a distance. We will consider just why people travel when social networks are more mobile and dispersed. Given the significance of much more extensive communication within contemporary societies, why are there still increasing amounts of physical travel? Why bother with the risks, uncertainties and frustrations of movement? What is it about face-to-face meetings that people spend considerable money and time on the road and in the air to be physically present with other people? We consider how people stay connected when physically separated and on the move. Is networked social life at-a-distance going to be more important in the future? If so, what are the implications for travel and transport?

Social Science Approaches

It is difficult to find satisfactory answers to such questions either within social science or transport research. Much social science research ignores the movement of people for work, friendship and family, leisure and pleasure. Despite the fact that: 'natives, people confined to and by the places to which they belong, unsullied by contact with a larger world, have probably never existed' (Appadurai 1988, 39), the social sciences mostly fail to examine how social life presupposes both the actual and the imagined movement of people from place to place, person to person, event to event. And yet migration, pilgrimages, war, trade, expeditions and colonization have linked most countries in complex travel connections. From early times servants, settlers, missionaries, soldiers, sailors, traders, scientists and many others travelled and formed extensive links across the world (Weber 1976; Bartlett 1993; Clifford 1997; Fennell 1997; de Vries and van der Woude 1997; Urry 2000).

Some social scientists regard mobility as producing a lack of connections, commitment, trust and emotional nearness (Albrow 1997; Cresswell 2002). Mobility undermines communities and 'social capital', as recently argued by Putnam (2000). Human geographers have argued that mobility destroys authentic senses of place by turning them into 'placeless' sites of speed and superficial consumption. As Tuan says: 'modern man might be so mobile that he can never establish roots and his experience of place may be all too superficial' (1977, 183). Relph argues in a similar fashion that:

> Roads, railways, airports, cutting across or imposed on the landscape rather than developing with it, are not only features of placelessness in their own right, but, by making the possible the mass movement of people with all their fashions and habits, have encouraged the spread of placelessness well beyond their immediate impacts. (cited in Cresswell 2002, 34)

George Simmel argued that people in the modern metropolis increasingly found themselves amongst strangers and they therefore had to learn the social skill of distancing themselves from the mobile crowd. Simmel adopted the figure of the stranger to illustrate the modern metropolis's unique geographies of proximity and distance: here people are close in a spatial sense, yet remote in a social sense. Simmel thus suggests that strangers are nearby while 'close ones' are likely to be distant (see discussion in Allen 2000, 57).

Overall the methods of the social sciences tend to emphasize everyday face-to-face proximities and interactions. For example, Sheldon's classic 1948 study of elderly people in Wolverhampton: 'defined a close relative as someone who lived within five minutes walking distance, being a measure of the distance a hot meal could be carried from one dwelling to another without reheating' (cited in Fennell 1997, 90). Successive studies of families, communities and social capital 'have followed this steer in taking *close* to mean *near* or interacting frequently face-to-face; and, by extension, significant, important, meaningful' (Fennell 1997, 90). Social science thus tends to focus upon ongoing and direct social interactions between peoples and social groups that constitute a proximate social structure. Travel is mostly seen as a neutral set of technologies and processes predominantly permitting forms of economic, social and political life explicable in terms of other, more causally powerful processes. Indeed, as we will see, research on social networks normally fails to analyse travel at all. Moreover, social science portrays communication as sequences of face-to-face-encounters in specific fixed physical spaces. We can say that social science in its analyses of communities, places and social life prefers to study *roots* rather than *routes* (Clifford 1997).

Transport Approaches

By contrast, transport planning and modelling mostly ignore the social dimensions of travel and the broader issues of how travel and transport help to produce modern societies. Transport researchers take the demand for transport as largely given, as a black box not needing much further investigation, or as derived from the level of a society's income. Also, transport researchers tend to examine simple categories of travel, such as commuting, leisure, or business, and presume that journeys have one purpose. Moreover, most transport research and modelling sees travel as individually shaped and chosen (through individual utility maximization), and they therefore have little understanding of how travel patterns are socially embedded and depend upon complex networks of family life, work and friendship.

Most travel-demand forecasts and the resulting transport strategies are based on the assumption that travellers demonstrate highly routine and predictable travel behaviour. Transport researchers tend to focus upon everyday commuting and peak hour traffic, partly because this causes most problems for transport system managers. They concentrate upon the representative day with its representative rush hour. This overlooks the high level of day-to-day variability in travel patterns (Schlich et al 2004), especially because leisure travel is at the individual level less consistent over time compared with commuting. Leisure travel is an important component of this intrapersonal variability and indeed more generally of changing travel patterns. Transport research does not adequately explain why so-called leisure travel is fundamental to many forms of social life.

Research Objectives

This book seeks to remedy social science and transport planning approaches through developing, along with other contributions, a social science of travel as it tries to insert analyses of the *social* within transport research and of *travel* within the social sciences. We explore changes in travel and communication through examining the changing patterns of people's social networks. We develop one of the first social science analyses of social networks, travel, communication and meetings.

While it seems that distances between members of networks have increased in the latter part of the twentieth century, not much transport research or social science research has systematically mapped such *social* networks *and* the associated networking practices. Partly inspired by Castells's focus upon financial and informational networks (1996), much network and mobility research has focused upon mobile professionals with many weak ties but apparently few strong ones (Ó Riain 2000; Wittel 2001; Kennedy 2004, 2005; Beaverstock 2005; Kesselring 2006; Lassen 2006). Simonsen argues: 'So issues of intersubjectivity, care and social connections – elements of everyday family lives – are conspicuous by their absence in such representations' (2003, 30). By contrast, this book explores, to use Conradson and Latham's term, 'middling' forms of mobile life (2005b, 229) and those *strong* ties to friends and family members. We examine to what degree dispersed ties and emotionally important networking at-a-distance are characteristic of many people other than the transnational elites and underprivileged migrants.

This book shows how there are five interdependent mobilities that form geographies of networks and mobilities in the contemporary world. These are:

- *Physical travel* of people for work, leisure, family life, pleasure, migration, and escape;
- *Physical movement* of objects delivered to producers, consumers and retailers;
- *Imaginative travel* elsewhere through images and memories seen on texts, TV, computer screens and film;
- *Virtual travel* on the internet;
- *Communicative travel* through person-to-person messages via letters, postcards, birthday and Christmas cards, telegrams, telephones, faxes, emails, instant messages, videoconferences and 'skyping'.

We deploy the concept of *network capital*, of cars, motorcycles, season tickets, phones, mobile phones, internet access points, and so on, showing how such capital is necessary for organizing and orchestrating networks especially of those ties that live beyond the reach of daily or weekly face-to-face relations. This form of capital makes the world spatially and temporally smaller by affording long bridges and fast connections between geographically dispersed people, partly because imaginative, virtual and communicative travel allows people to be in a sense in two or more places at once. Most social research focuses upon one of these separate mobilities, such as passenger transport or mobile telephony or the internet, and generalizes from that. This book, by contrast, examines the interconnections between these different mobilities central to the making and maintaining of near and of faraway network ties.[1]

---

1   It should be noted that this book understands friendships, families and communities, as well as businesses and professions, as social networks. 'Travel' is used here to refer to the physical movement of people. By 'communication' we refer to various forms of face-to-

We examine how social networks are spatially distributed and how they are produced through networking practices of travel, communications and meetings in apparently mobile societies. Social networks involve technologies and work, there is networking through travel, communication and meetings. We will examine how, and where, they do network and make networks come to life through emailing friends and email lists, text messaging friends about parties, gossiping on the phone, cruising at receptions, chatting over a coffee, going for a drink and spending hours on the road and/or in the air between recurrent meetings (see also Conradson and Latham 2005b). And we explore the geographies of these networking technologies and practices: how much physical, virtual or imaginative travel do they entail, and over how long a distance?

We look at how networks have to meet up intermittently in order to cement their connections, to enjoy each other's company and to carry out certain obligations. We hypothesize that in more-distributed societies with connections at-a-distance and people being less likely to bump into their contacts, scheduled visits and meetings are highly significant (Axhausen 2005b). Transport and meetings at-a-distance seem increasingly necessary and obligatory to social life, not only as commuting to work, but as leisure activities or through attendance at birthdays, weddings, funerals, or visits to friends and family members. Much travel demand seems to stem from a powerful 'compulsion to proximity', to feel the need to be physically co-present and to fulfil social and cultural obligations with significant others (sometimes against one's will: Boden and Molotch 1994; Urry 2003). So this book explores the *social* obligations that result in various kinds of demand for physical travel.

This book pays much attention to what extent communications are enhancing and/or substituting for physical travel. We explore how travel and meetings are spatially and temporally coordinated, how people use websites, emails, text messages, mobile calls to synchronize complex preferences, diaries, travel routes and time schedules before and during meetings. Travel and meetings require systems of coordination and mobile communication technologies that enable dispersed network members to coordinate co-presence in-between meetings. Further, we consider how communication technologies may on occasions substitute for physical face-to-face meetings and hence travel. We briefly explore the significance of new and future ways of meeting up that do not involve physical travel and co-presence but rather virtual co-presence and communicative travel.

---

interface-to-face communications such as the movement of images, texts, sounds and words through faxing, emailing, text messaging, messaging, videoconferencing, speaking on the phone or the net ('skyping', see www.skype.com). We use the term 'meeting' to refer to the planned or unplanned physical co-presence of two or more people who in some sense orient their actions to each other (and not just to business or professional-type meetings). Some meetings involve meeting up with particular classes of people, members of a particular organization, profession, family and so on. We use the term 'virtual meeting' to refer to various forms of mediated and virtual co-presence effected through one or more means of communications, either one-to-many or one-to-one.

In particular we examine to what extent a small but carefully chosen sample of youngish people in the North-West of England have dispersed network geographies. Are their links predominately nearby or faraway? How far do they live from the people that are important to them? How often do they meet, talk over long distances and communicate with their strong ties and to what degree does distance determine regularity? So when we speak of geographies of social networks we explore how people have moved about over time and how they network spatially (close by, faraway, staying put, on the move, on the phone or the internet, etc.) *and* temporally (everyday, weekly, at weekends or holidays, etc.) with specific ties.

Mobile methods

This research project employs and develops mobile methods, by contrast with the methods of social science that are normally a-mobile[2] as they emphasize everyday face-to-face interactions and short-distance mobility (Larsen, Axhausen and Urry 2006; Sheller and Urry 2006). So, until recently there has been a neglect of long-distance travel, occasional sociality and mediated communication. However, if friends and family members no longer live near each other, the regular 'dropping-in' type of visits becomes difficult. And when friends and family members do meet up each visit is likely to last longer (and involve staying over). We hypothesize that *ceteris paribus* the greater the distance between people who meet up, the longer the time that meetings will last. People may thus compensate for the intermittent nature and generalized transport cost of visits (time, money and weariness) by spending a whole day or weekend or week(s) together in each other's company, often staying in each other's homes (this may have implications for household and furniture size and design). While McGlone, Park and Roberts (1999, 146) document that friends and families socialize less often at each other's houses, this is not the same as a general fall in friendship and family visits.

We noted that transport studies with their conventional one-day travel data privilege repetitive everyday mobility and by implication relative short-distance travel. If we only observe everyday mobility (within a short period of time) we will conclude that most people live relative localised lives. Thus a recent study concludes that Swedish families live localized lives because their everyday transport patterns are local and revolve around private homes (Ellegård and Wilhelmson 2004). Yet if the researchers had also had examined occasional long-distance travel and weekend touring, to visit friends or family members or tourist sites, their conclusions may not have been the same. Indeed, three transport studies have used six-week travel

---

2   Mobile methods mean two things. Firstly, they are methods where the researcher also moves along with the people, images or objects that are moving and are being studied (see Marcus 1998; Bærenholdt, Haldrup, Larsen and Urry 2004). Secondly, the methods can be mobile by capturing through observation, questionnaires, interviews, mapping and traces, the complex mobilities of the people, images and objects under study (see Sheller and Urry 2006). This project mainly uses mobile methods in the second sense.

diaries to show that travel practices of households incorporate not only routines but also 'detours' and new destinations, especially over the weekend (if these studies had taken place over the summer holiday months, the significance of variety-seeking and long-distance journeys would have been even more marked) (Schlich et al 2004; Schönfelder and Axhausen 2004). The social life of most people during the week is bound up with a specific locality and short trips while many embark on longer journeys such as leisure activities, sightseeing and visiting friends and family, at weekends, festival holidays and other holidays.

Mobile methods highlight how research should analyse those processes by which co-presence and intimacy are on occasions brought about, and the socialities involved when people are not involved in daily interactions with each other but with whom a sense of connection is sensed and sustained. If social networks are becoming more dispersed and people are less able to visit one another on a daily or even weekly basis, then we cannot equate closeness and communion with geographical nearness and daily or weekly co-present visits. Long-distance leisurely travel (albeit often very hectic) is important to research for its social and emotional significance. Despite being less frequent, long-distance travel can be as significant as everyday short-distance trips.

In the past much leisure travel could have been classified as *touristic* and by implication unnecessary. But now it seems that affordable, reliable and well-connected tourist-type travel is necessary for friendship and family life, social inclusion and social capital. We examine to what degree leisure travel involves reconnecting with friends and family members living elsewhere, rather than only seeing new and interesting places. We label this tourism proximity and suggest that visiting friends and relatives (VFR) tourism is an important contemporary element of travel and one increasing in significance.

Mobile methods are distinct from typical transport research by highlighting how studies of the physical movement of people and objects must be supplemented by studies of imaginative, virtual and communication travel. We are also concerned with the methods used to research the *socialities* involved in communications, by letter, phone, email and text message, that take place in-between physical meetings. Even people living in localized fashion may be in frequent conversation with distant connections through letters, telephone calls, emails and text messages. It is necessary to examine caring at-a-distance as well as socializing at-a-distance to redefine further conventional notions of what it is to be *close*. As Fennell describes about a time before the mobile phone:

> Take 73-year old Grace Angel, who was born in Wandsworth and has lived in her house in Tooting [London] for over fifty years ... She engages in all the traditional activities of a settled life; visiting family, knitting and enjoying crafts. She rarely leaves Wandsworth; she enjoys the sense of community ... At the same time her life is not confined by the locality. She tells how she writes letters to France and the United States. (1997, 45)

Similarly, people and groups who may seem isolated can be in frequent face-to-interface-to-face contact with significant others living elsewhere. Thus the apparent decline in the frequency of physically visiting people may be compensated for by an increase in the frequency of communicating by phone and through SMS messaging and emails. We argue that mobile methods should analyse how people simultaneously lead local lives and possess distant ties, how they sustain ties through virtual and imaginative travel as well as through face-to-face interaction.

Like Harvey's notion of 'time–space compression', mobile methods must see space and time as interconnected (see also Pred 1977; May and Thrift 2001). New transport and communication technologies not only result in 'time–space compression' or the 'death of distance' (see Cairncross 1997), but also of increasing distance in order to meet up with one's network. Sometimes people can make connections at-a-distance in a few seconds while at other times they spend hours or days in cars, trains and planes just to see their close friends and relatives for brief moments. Two friends emailing between the UK and Pakistan are only a cheap email away but the distances separating them materialize bodily when they move in and out of bus stations, train platforms, airport lounges and are confined to narrow seats for many hours. Even though travel time and travel cost (especially in relation to European air travel) has shrunk within the last decade, the friction of distance and the cost of travel do matter in relation to physical travel that is now often necessary to meet up with distant network contacts. 'Time–space compression' can thus paradoxically involve more spatially dispersed social networks that are harder to reach. There can be an increasing 'travel burden' (Shove 2002).

And mobile methods need to be *relational*. This book demonstrates that much research overemphasizes individualized networking and overlooks the relational commitments that people have to their social networks (Conradson and Latham 2005a). People are involved in social dramas wherein actions depend upon negotiation, approval and feelings, and have social and emotional consequences. Individuals are part of networks that both enable and constrain possible individual actions. They are immobilized and mobilized in complex relational ways. Yet much travel and tourism theory has seen travellers as free-floating individuals seeking to maximize *their* aspirations. Such theory fails to notice the social obligations and burdens of apparently *free* mobility (but see Urry 2002; Coles, Duvall and Hall 2005; Hall 2005). This book demonstrates how there are various more or less binding and more or less pleasurable social obligations that require intermittent face-to-face co-presence.

Overview

Drawing upon much existing research, mobile methods and the data analysed, this book develops methods, general hypotheses and theories that can be subsequently employed in conjunction with a large sample. Thus the stage will be set for substantive future research that would entail a large-scale survey of social networks and mobilities (for some detail, see Chapter 9).

To provide a context for the empirical work, we first examine existing theories and research. Chapter 2 examines the main analyses of social networks; we argue for a 'mobility ties approach' that understands social networks as mobile and performed, having to be practised to be meaningful and durable. Chapter 3 reviews literature that is concerned with why face-to-face meetings are fundamental to social networks, and we make the argument that much tourist-type travel is as much about sociability as about the search for the 'exotic'. In Chapter 4 we set out the five main forms of mobility and specifically examine the physical movement of people, showing some of the connections with the other mobilities. We show how communication technologies are central to coordinating meetings and travel. Chapter 5 discusses in some detail the methodological framing of our empirical research, and how it might be improved upon in subsequent studies.

Our empirical work is reported in three parts. In Chapter 6 we develop methods that help us to analyse the spatial–temporal patterns of people's social networks. We test and employ methods that measure and map networks. In the following chapter we examine the role that the increasing amount of tourist-type travel plays in societies where social life is conducted at-a-distance. We analyse how people visit and receive the hospitality of close friends, workmates and family members living elsewhere. This helps us to understand the spatial patterns of people's social networks. In this chapter we examine the social obligations involved in attending Christmas parties, birthdays, weddings, funerals and so on. Chapter 8 examines how physical travel and communicative travel fold into each other, and especially how email and mobile phone calls and SMS texting often enhance the nature of travel. We look at how respondents coordinate travel and co-presence through the Internet, email and mobile phone communications with network members living close by and especially faraway.

The final chapter draws together our analysis of 'networking for life' and examines some implications for both future research and the future of travel and transport.

Chapter 2

Social Networks

Introduction

This chapter reviews the main analyses of social networks in the modern world: the community studies and the social capital approach, social network analysis, and the small worlds approach. We then argue for a *mobilities approach* that understands social networks as mobile and performed, having to be practised to be meaningful and durable. Networks should be viewed as an accomplishment, involving and made possible through various network tools such as cars, buses, trains, planes, laptops, networked computers, personal organizers, mobile phones, text messages and so on. Subsequently we briefly review various empirical studies of the networking practices of mobile professionals, long-distance relationships, fragmented families and diasporic families. Here we argue that much social scientific mobility research works with the notion of autonomous, free-floating individuals and thereby overlooks the relational economies of commitments and obligations to family members, partners and friends that connect people and their networks.

Community Studies and Social Capital

We begin with the classic study by Hoggart who, in writing about a 1930s urban setting, argues: 'The core of working class attitudes ... is a sense of the personal, the concrete, the local ... first the family and second the neighbourhood'. Later he argues that within 'the massed proletarian areas' there are 'small worlds, each as homogenous and well-defined as a village where one knows practically everybody, an extremely local life, in which everything is remarkably near' (both cited in Albrow 1997, 40). Although not all community studies have portrayed communities as so tight-knit, Hoggart illustrates that community studies have looked for social networks and their structures of support, friendship, kinship, place attachment and intimacy as located within particular physically confined localities, such as neighbourhoods.

To develop a more suitable analytical framework, Bell and Newby distinguish three notions of community (1976). First, there is community based upon close geographical propinquity, but where there is no implication of the quality or even presence of the social relationships found in such settlements of co-presence. Second, there is the sense of community as the local social system in which there is a relatively bounded set of systemic interrelationships of social groups and local institutions. Third, there is communion, human association characterized by close personal ties, belongingness, and a strong sense of duty and obligation between its members. Bell and Newby show that no particular settlement type necessarily produces communion. It can occur where those involved do not dwell in close physical proximity. Geographical propinquity also does not necessitate a local social system, nor does localness necessarily generate communion. It follows that we can have communities without close-knit and interacting social networks and social networks of communion that move across specific places. Yet the social sciences have overly focused upon geographically propinquitous communities based on more or less face-to-face social interactions with those routinely present.

This last orientation can be seen in Putnam's influential US research in *Bowling Alone* (2000). Putnam argues that good communities depend upon rich and multilayered forms of social capital; this 'refers to connections among individuals – social networks and norms of reciprocity and trustworthiness that arise from them' (Putnam 2000, 19). Communities in the USA with substantial social capital are characterized by dense networks of reciprocal social relations, well-developed sets of mutual obligations, generalized reciprocity, high levels of trust in one's neighbours, overlapping conversational groupings and bonds that bridge across conventional social divides. Putnam also believes that civic-minded and well-integrated communities are essential for economic prosperity and growth. Social bonds and especially involvement in civic work within neighbourhoods are considered crucial to social capital, and it is local face-to-face socializing, church going, political rallying, volunteer work, philanthropy, general trust and reciprocity that have been in decline since the start of the last third of the twentieth century. Strong ties of local communities are fading. American people are less connected, they are likely to be strangers to their neighbours, they have less co-present face-to-face talk and they show little local civic engagement.

In addition to generational changes, Putnam argues that the widespread growth of TV, urban sprawl and travel are major causes of these changes. TV 'privatizes leisure time … TV watching comes at the expense of nearly every social activity outside the home, especially social gatherings and informal conversations' (Putnam 2000, 236–7). Slum clearance programmes of the 1950s and 1960s also destroyed those close-knit community ties that involved intensive short-range corporeal mobility (Putnam 2000, 281). America's liking for residential mobility is detrimental to social capital:

> Just as frequent movers have weaker community ties, so too communities with higher rates of residential turnover are less well integrated. Mobile communities seem less friendly to their inhabitants than do their more stable communities. Crime rates are higher, and school performances are lower, in high-mobility communities. In such communities, even longtime residents have fewer ties with their neighbors. So mobility undermines civic engagement and community-based social capital. (2000, 204–5)

Putnam notes how two-thirds of car trips involve driving alone and this is growing; the time and distance of solitary work commutes is increasing; each additional minute in daily commuting time reduces involvement in community affairs by both commuters and non-commuters; and spatial fragmentation between home and workplace is especially bad for community groups that historically straddled class, ethnic and gender divides (2000, 212–14).

Putnam outlines how to reverse declining local social capital. One suggestion is that: 'Let us act to ensure that by 2010 Americans will spend less time traveling and more time connecting with our neighbors than we do today, that we will live in more integrated and pedestrian-friendly areas, and that the design of our communities and the availability of public space will encourage more casual socializing with friends and neighbors' (Putnam 2000, 407–8). Putnam's approach to community building and social capital has influenced the UK government's Innovation and Performance Unit, where one working paper states:

> Geographic mobility can have a detrimental impact upon social capital. Residential mobility breaks up social networks and lessens social contact between friends and family. Relationships that depend on face to face contact - such as informal eldercare and childcare – may suffer from increased mobility. (Donovan, Pilch and Rubenstein 2002, 3)

Putnam is not without critics. Some accuse him of being nostalgic in his concentration upon organized leisure such as bowling, Scout troops and church going. While participation in some such traditional institutions has fallen, newer groups such as pub-based soccer clubs and environmental NGOs are flourishing. This can also be seen in the UK where the Kendal study showed declining church and chapel attendance, at the same time as the growth of participation in many new age and 'spiritual' associations and movements (Heelas et al 2005).

Overall Costa and Hahnthere indicate that there is only a small decline in joining groups and no fall in socialising with friends and family members in the evening (reported in Florida 2002, 269–70). Watters (2004) challenges Putnam's derogatory view on friendships and his heroic view of civic organizations. According to Putnam, friends ('schmoozers') are only concerned with inwardly focused bonding while civic work is concerned with noble outwardly focused bridging. So schmoozers are causing a decline in civic engagement and therefore a fall in social capital. But Watters reminds us that meetings in Lions Clubs are not only concerned with altruistic, civic matters but also with plain old schmoozing and business networking, and that tight-knit communities often are static, conservative and exclusive. That is, they bond rather than bridge (Watters 2004; see also Florida 2002, 269–70).

Florida, indeed, shows how social networks of friends among youngish (unmarried) city-dwellers can generate much social capital, now that people enter family life at a later stage and are less likely to do traditional civic work. Certainly, amongst 'the creative class', youngish well-educated people prefer tolerant and diverse communities of weak ties and do wish to escape Putnam's tight-knit small-town communities (Florida 2002, 269). Florida further argues that 'creative capital' rather than social capital is emerging as crucial for prosperity in contemporary informational economies.

The final point to note is that Putnam's notion of social capital is at odds with more recent community research that travels beyond local cultures to deconstruct ideas of local cultures, static social networks and fixed places (Albrow 1997; Albrow et al

1997; Durrschmidt 1997; Urry 2000). On this account places are seen as constructed through, as Clifford (1997) says, routes as well as roots. Or as Massey puts it: 'what gives a place its specificity is not some long internalized history but the fact that it is constructed out of particular constellation of relations articulated together at a particular locus' (1994, 217). Communities are impure and porous. Travel is central to communities, even to those characterized by relatively high levels of apparent propinquity and communion.

Social Network Analysis (SNA)

In this section we examine SNA through the extensive research programme of Wellman and collaborators at Toronto. SNA is concerned with mapping the links between people, organizations, interest groups, places, and so on. It takes as its starting point the assumption that social life, beneath all its apparent messiness, randomness and chaos, is networked, a larger structured web of social connections strung between people and technologies, near and far. In this sense, SNA is concerned with uncovering, rendering visible, already existing networks, their links and properties. It can involve a mathematical analysis of relationships often stretching across distance, and is grounded in mainly quantitative empirical data (see Scott 2000, for a related UK-focused review).

Wellman notes that communities always have and will continue to pervade social existence. In fact, wherever SNA has looked, communities are flourishing (Hampton and Wellman 2001; Wellman 2001, 2002; Wellman and Haythornthwaite 2002; Boase and Wellman 2004). The reason why commentators like Putnam have found a dearth of communities is because they have looked for communities in the wrong places, in neighbourhoods and localities, the traditional sites.[1] Indeed when Wellman talks of communities there are few traces of civic connections and normative expectations. He does not lament the demise of communities because North Americans no longer bowl in leagues, participate in mainstream political campaigns, join neighbourhood associations and regularly attend chapel or church (although Americans do attend those more than any other society in the developed world).

SNA explores the structural properties that connect people in webs of friendship, mutual support and sociality through face-to-face talk, phone conversations and email. SNA illustrates how communities and social capital are tied into and dependent upon technological cultures and virtual spaces: 'Rather than being exclusively online or in-line, many community ties are complex dances of face-to-face encounters, scheduled meetings, two-person telephone calls, emails to one person or several, and broader online discussion among those sharing interests' (Wellman 2001, 237). Network ties exist in and across both physical space and various virtual or cyberspaces (Wellman 2001, Wellman and Haythornthwaite 2002). Thus communities are in flux, transforming and even developing on the move within loose networks:

---

1   However it should be noted here that Putnam and Wellman strangely only sporadically refer to each other.

> We find community in networks, not groups ... In networked societies: boundaries are permeable, interactions are with diverse others, connections switch between multiple networks, and hierarchies can be flatter and recursive ... Communities are far-flung, loosely-bounded, sparsely-knit and fragmentary. Most people operate in multiple, thinly-connected, partial communities as they deal with networks of kin, neighbours, friends, workmates and organizational ties. Rather than fitting into the same group as those around them, each person his/her own personal community. (Wellman 2001, 227)

So communities are found in networks, and such networked communities are not confined to a particular place but are stretched out geographically and socially. Moreover, in 'networked societies' people are tied into multiple networks. Each person is uniquely connected to diverse networks, so each possesses a 'personal community'. Communities, these interpersonal ties of sociality, support, information and identity, are far-flung and individualized (Wellman 2001, 228).

Wellman captures these shifts as involving transformations from *door-to-door* to *place-to-place* to *person-to-person* communities. First, people walking to visit each other typify door-to-door communities that were spatially compact and densely knit; 'little boxes' based upon geographical propinquity (Wellman 2002). This is the kind of community that Putnam yearns for. Family life in at least parts of Europe and North America in the first half of the twentieth century was probably lived within such a 'little box' with family members regularly encountering each other within their immediate neighbourhood. There was an informal co-presence of family members. Classic studies that documented this up to the 1950s were conducted in the East End of London and various Italian-American 'urban villages' (Gans 1962; Young and Willmott 1962). Significant others were encountered through walking about such neighbourhoods, through what Wellman terms door-to-door connectivity (2001, 231). People walked or cycled to visit one another and there was much overlap of family life, work and friendship. According to Wellman, door-to-door communities expired with the increased speed of transport and especially communications: 'huge increase[s] in speed [have] made door-to-door communications residual, and made most communications place-to-place or person-to-person' (2001, 233).

Second, with 'place-to-place' communities, interactions move inside the private home; it is here that entertaining, phone calls and emails take place: 'the household is what is visited, telephoned or emailed' (Wellman 2001, 234). Yet this is not seen as destroying networks and social capital, because phone calls and emails connect homes in disparate geographical locations and produce communion with those who do not live close by. The house is a site not only of TV consumption and inward bonding, but also of communicating with near and distant acquaintances. Against the thesis that the internet makes social networks disembodied and virtual, Wellman's studies suggest that 'computer mediated communication supplements, arranges and amplifies in-person and telephone communication rather than replacing them' (2001, 242; Hampton and Wellman 2001; see also Castells 2001). Those who are on-line are those who are most active in voluntary and political work within their immediate neighbourhood (Wellman 2001, 10). The internet increases local as well as long-distance involvement (Wellman 2001, 236). While the internet offers global access and connectivity, most emails are local and concerned with local arrangements, sustaining contact with familiar faces and arranging and rescheduling face-to-face meetings (Wellman 2001, 236; Boase and Wellman 2004). 'Frequent contact on the Internet is a complement to frequent face-to-face contact, not a substitute for it' (Wellman, cited in Putnam 2000, 179). A study of American college students showed that 64 per cent of them used face-to-face, telephone and the internet to conduct their social life. Only 2 per cent relied solely upon face-to-face connections (Byam, Zhang and Lin 2004, 306).

Third, with person-to-person community, the person 'has become the portal' (Wellman 2001, 238). The turn to person-to-person results from innovations in communications; according to Wellman: 'the technological development of computer-communication and the societal flourish of social networks are now affording the rise of *networked individualism*' (2002, 2; see also Castells 2001). Whereas the emblematic technology of place-to-place connectivity was the fixed landline telephone, the mobile phone is the technology of person-to-person communities. 'Mobile phones afford a fundamental liberation from place, and they soon will be joined by wireless computers and personalized software' (Wellman 2001, 238). While landlines eliminated the prerequisite of physical proximity, they reinforced the need to be at specific places. Personalized, wireless worlds afford networked individualism, each person is, so to say, the engineer of his/her own ties and networks, and always connected (technology permitting!), no matter where she/he is going and staying. Person-to-person brings about what Wellman calls 'mobile-ization' that 'suits and reinforces mobile lifestyles and physically dispersed relationships' (2001, 239). Or as Licoppe reports: 'the mobile phone is portable, to the extent of seeming to be an extension of its owner, a personal object constantly there, at hand ... Wherever they go, individuals seem to carry their network of connections which could be activated telephonically at any moment' (2004, 139). The mobile phone frees people from much spatial fixity (Geser 2004, 4).

Central to this notion of 'networked individualism' is that friendships and networks are chosen and specific. People know and socialize with an increasing number of friends, workmates and 'networks', but these relationships are specialized in the sense that they revolve around particular roles, skills, leisure pursuits, places and sites; they dissolve if they cease to satisfy these functions (Wellman 2002, 6). Networked individualism can produce many weak rather than strong ties. As Granovetter (1983) has taught us, bonds and ties come both as weak and strong; most people have strong ties with a few people (partner, parents, best friend and so on) and weak(er) links with a larger group of people. Weak links are crucial for linking different networks, and Granovetter speaks of them as bridges: weak links bridge once-separated networks in the same fashion as bridges connect once-separated pieces of land and people. Such weak ties connect people to the outside world, providing a bridge other than that provided by close friends and family. Without bridges communities would degrade into isolated small worlds of cliques.

Networks are said to be increasingly individualized, part of a wider individualization of 'reflexive modern societies'. Wellman's notion of 'networked individualism' has much in common with the individualization theses of Giddens (1994) and Beck. To cite the latter:

> We live in an age in which the social order of the national state, class, ethnicity and the traditional family is in decline. The ethic of individual self-fulfilment and achievement is the most powerful current in modern societies. The choosing, deciding, shaping human being who aspires to be the author of his or her own life, the creator of an individual identity, is the central character of our time. (2001, 165)

'The individual as actor' is the 'designer, juggler and stage director of his own biography, identity, social networks, commitments and convictions' (Beck 2001, 166).

From our viewpoint Wellman and his collaborators' work focused on communications through the internet and mobile telephony while paying limited attention to travel and the detailed spatial distribution of network members (this is true of SNA more generally). This is striking, given the attention as to how communication technologies connect people in order to arrange future off-line meetings. There has been less attention paid to how people attend such meetings, where they are located and how much travel they entail. There could have been greater examination of how trains, buses, cars and airplanes fit into the shifts from 'door-to-door' to 'place-to-place' to 'person-to-person' relations. We will subsequently ask how travel produces and stabilizes distributed networks, as indeed Wellman and his collaborators are now developing in their *Connected Lives* project (Wellman et al 2005).

Small World Analysis

A related approach to social network research is the recent *small world analysis*, which, among other things, attempts to explain mathematically the so-called 'small world phenomenon' (see Urry 2004b, on the following). Watts (2003) developed an explanation of the empirical finding demonstrated by various researchers that all people on the planet, whatever their social location, are separated by about six degrees of separation. It is common for people who believe that they are strangers to each other to find that they are in fact connected along a quite short chain of acquaintanceship. Watts argues that: 'even when two people do not have a friend in common they are separated by only a short chain of intermediaries' (2003, 4; Barabàsi 2002, 27–30). A small world experience refers to these intermittent occasions where one bumps into an apparently stranger that turns out to 'know' one's partner's parents' best friend or workmate. Small world meetings are particularly powerful when away – the farther away – from home. It is this apparently strange small world phenomenon that various authors seek to explain by modelling networks on the edge of order and randomness. They share with SNA the ontological assumption that social life is fundamentally networked.

Small world analysis is also inspired by Granovetter's analysis of the strength of weak ties (1983). He shows that extensive weak ties of acquaintanceship and informational flow are central to successful job searches and, by implication, to many other social processes such as the spreading of jokes and rumours. Granovetter's findings suggest that strong links do not exist in isolation but form triangles. If somehow a strong link should disappear from the network, two steps would still be enough to go from one end to the other. In ordered isolated networks where each person is connected to, say, his or her 50 nearest neighbours, then there would be 60 million degrees of separation in order to go even halfway around the world (Buchanan 2002, 114).

If, though, there are just a few long-range random ties or weak links connecting each of these clumps of 50 neighbours, then the degree of separation dramatically drops, from 60 million to five (Barabàsi 2002). So it is weak ties – these long-distance bridges – that are responsible for creating the small worlds, for bringing geographically dispersed people into much lower degrees of separation from each other. Watts then shows that a wide array of phenomena, from the networks of film stars to electric power interconnections, demonstrates a similar patterning, a combination of tight clumps with a few random long-term connections.

However, while Watts' and other writings are full of anecdotes about random meetings in foreign places,[2] they discuss small worlds without taking account of the mechanisms of travel, communications and especially meetings that may generate long-term connections (but see Dodds, Muhamed and Duncan 2003). Small worlds, it appears, are universal phenomena of social relationships; they exist in pre-modern and modern worlds with equal force. Wherever people happen to live they are only a short chain of intermediaries away from anyone else (Buchanan 2002, 35). These authors explain small worlds through mathematical abstraction; they prove that in any society (whatever scale) with just a few weak social ties or bridges (so basically all societies) no person is more than six degrees from any other person.

While the six degrees of separation thesis is intriguing, it is those links – direct and indirect – within one or two steps of separation that seem crucial for most peoples' patterns of everyday life (Watters 2004, 105). Such connections between people presuppose intermittent meetings. They are not cost free. Although people may 'know' others in a short chain of acquaintanceship, this will produce less affect than if they intermittently meet. Indeed in some senses people might be said only to 'know' each other if they do meet intermittently (although it might be that intense meetings at one time, say as students, can then carry the relationship without so many further meetings). Also it would seem that those with the largest number of

---

2   To cite Buchanan:

As for myself, I moved a few years ago from the United States to London … A few weeks after arriving, I went to a party with some new friends. At the party, most people were British, but quite by chance I sat next to a man who had come from the United States. From where, I asked? Oddly enough, Virginia, the very same state where I had been living. From where in Virginia? Remarkably, Charlottesvile, the not-very-large town from which I too had just come. Where had he lived in Charlottesville? Well, as it turned out, on the same street as myself, just a few doors down, even though I had never met him before. (2002, 24)

weak ties will tend to be advantaged in such meetings, so producing many more weak ties.

We might thus suggest that a network only functions if it is intermittently 'activated' through occasioned co-presence. *Ceteris paribus*, 'network activation' occurs if there are periodic events each week, or month or year when meeting is more or less obligatory. And meetings involve massive amounts of physical travel. Social networks are, it seems, less coherent with fewer overlapping multiple affiliations, people's residences and activities are spatially more distributed and when people do meet face-to-face this normally involves longer-distance travel. In 1800 in the USA people on average travelled 50 metres a day – now they travel 50 kilometres a day (Buchanan 2002: 121).

Small world analysis thus never really examines how links are organized and reinforced through specific meetings and travel to connect with particular weak and strong ties. So Buchanan reports that each 'social network has not been designed by anyone. It has evolved through countless historical accidents – people meeting people by chance' (Buchanan 2002, 41). But such meetings are often not by chance but by design, as the fourth approach here tries to examine in depth.

Mobilities Approach

Departing from and elaborating upon the three approaches just reviewed, this project develops a fourth approach to social networks based upon the systematic examination of physical, imaginative and virtual travel *and* of their interdependencies (Sheller and Urry 2006). This mobilities approach argues that extensive regional, national and transitional flows and meetings of objects, technologies, representations and people (may) produce small worlds. Bridges are crucial, but so are the traffic, the meeting-places and greetings along these bridges. It examines how this traffic can take place through cars, buses, trains and airplanes, and through letters, emails, telephone calls, photographs, websites and videoconferences. These 'network tools' of 'network capital' (Axhausen 2005b) make the world smaller by affording long bridges and fast connections between geographically dispersed people, and between people and places. Social networks involve diverse connections, which are more or less at-a-distance, more or less intense and more or less mobile. There are thus material worlds that organize and orchestrate networks, especially those ties that lie beyond the daily or weekly face-to-face relations. Human practices and social networks are moreover intricately networked with extensive material worlds, with various technologies, machines, software, texts, objects, databases and so on that organize the very nature of social life (Licoppe and Smoreda 2005; see also Haldrup and Larsen 2006).

The mobilities approach suggests that what is important is not the absolute number of links that people possess; this is a rather abstract issue. Rather *meetingness* – talking, writing, emailing, travelling and visiting – is crucial to the nature of networks. Although people may know others in a short chain of acquaintanceship, this produces less consequence than if they intermittently meet, face-to-face, as well as encountering each other on the phone, texting and emailing. Central to networks are the form and character of meetings and hence of travel in order both to establish and to nourish links or at least temporarily cement them. Instead of focusing upon the formal structures of the networks themselves, this mobilities approach analyses the embodied making of networks, performances and practices of networking. Social networks come to life and are sustained through various practices of networking through email, forwarding messages, texting, sharing gossip, performing meetings, making two-minutes' bumping-into-people conversations, attending conferences, cruising at receptions, chatting over a coffee, meeting up for a drink and spending many hours on trains or on the road or in the air to meet up with business partners, clients, and displaced friends, family members, workmates and partner.

For example, Watters discusses how one-to-one and one-to-many emails particularly helped to bond his network:

> We constantly keep track of each other in a never-ending e-mail thread. On an average week, among my group of friends, there were hundreds of one-to-one e-mails, a dozen group e-mails, and perhaps fifty phone calls exchanged. I couldn't vouch for any deeper meaning in any of these communications or activities, but I could tell you that the subtext of almost all of them was a clear message of solidarity. That repeated message, from the group to the individual, was 'We're on your side'. (2004, 38)

Networking is effectively work, sometimes tedious and tiring, sometimes enjoyable and stimulating. The mobilities approach understands social networks as something accomplished, in process, weaving together the material and the social as well as pleasures, obligations and burdens. Travel, meetings, writing and talk make networks come intermittently to life. Physical travel is especially important in facilitating those co-present conversations, to the making of links and social connections, albeit unequal, that endure over time. Such connections derived from co-presence can generate relations of trust that enhance both social and economic inclusion. However, to be lacking in various networking tools (low in what we will call network capital) reduces the range and practices of travel. Interventions that reduce, channel or limit such mobilities weaken social capital and generate social exclusion (see Cass, Shove and Urry 2005).

We now briefly discuss some ethnographic research concerned with networking as accomplishment and practice, of building and maintaining social ties in mobile *network societies*. We start by analysing studies of transnational information work and continue by discussing research on family life on the move and at-a-distance. We call this *networking for a living* and *networking for life*. It will become evident that these two sets of network practices often overlap.

Mobile Workers and Global Workplaces

In *The Rise of the Network Society* (1996) Castells outlines a global analysis of the 'Information Age'. This informational economy is global as it works on a planetary scale in real time, and it is networked in that the connectivity of this global economy is sustained through the organisational idea of the network enterprise.

Wittel in his study of new media workers in London explores what kind of sociality flourishes amongst the 'avant-garde' of this Information Age. He uses the notion of 'network sociality'. By contrast with traditional closed societies based around mutual experiences and shared histories, network sociality is an open, individualized and mobile sociality of integration, disintegration and quick exchanges of information (Wittel 2001, 51). Thus:

> Network sociality is a technological sociality insofar as it is deeply embedded in communication technology, transport technology and technologies to manage relationships. It is a sociality that is based on the use of cars, trains, buses and the underground, of airplanes, taxis and hotels, and it is based on phones, faxes, answering machines, voicemail, videoconferencing, mobiles, email, chat rooms, discussion forums, mailing lists and web sites. Transportation and communication technologies provide the infrastructure for people and societies on the move. (Wittel 2001, 69–70)

Sociality among the sampled mobile urban media workers is fleeting and transient, intense and energetic. Wittel argues:

> Mobility and speed seem to be the primary reasons for this shift from a narrative- or experience-based sociality to an informational sociality. Mobility is important because more and more people are on the move and thus somewhere else. In order to re-establish social contacts, 'catching up' becomes an indispensable condition of social situations. Catching up is essentially informational. And the acceleration of speed in social encounters is additionally feeding the development towards an informational sociality. (2001, 52)

These media workers 'see' and 'know' a lot of people and new people speedily travel in and out of their private and professional lives. In this network sociality there are few strangers, only potential members of people's ever-expanding networks. This quick exchange of contacts commodifies personal relationships, according to Wittel. Network practices of managing relationships are performed through communication and transport technologies, as well as through face-to-face networking events where work and play are blurred: 'working practices become increasingly networking practices' (Wittel 2001, 53). London has a broad range of networking places where new media people meet up to show their face, catch up and exchange information, business cards, rumours, deals, greetings and glances. This takes place at specific networking events, receptions and informally in pubs, wine bars, cafes, clubs and restaurants. Wittel's analysis suggests a proliferation of urban places of cool, playful meetings where members of social milieux bump into each other, do business and have fun.

The mobile and networked character of networked sociality in the information economy is also examined in Kennedy's study of transnational architects and engineers (2004, 2005). He examines how these highly mobile workers sustain and not least form social networks of both weak and strong ties while on the move, moving from short-term project to short-term project. Kennedy's research suggests that such professional 'global nomads' produce and sustain different kinds of networks compared with migrants and members of diasporas. The latter depend upon support from family as they construct multistranded social relations linking together their new and old environments.

By contrast, global professionals normally go overseas alone on contract and move into cosmopolitan environments less influenced by national cultures (Kennedy 2004, 162). Their social networks consist of like-minded cosmopolitan workmates. They do not think of themselves as company people since their primary loyalty is to their profession. Companies are partly chosen because they demonstrate a 'cosmopolitan culture'. These people primarily participate in localized, small-scale transnational networks constructed around occupational links while on an assignment. Their leisure time is spent with workmates and friends (Kennedy 2004, 164). But, in a somewhat similar way to immigrants and diasporic cultures, these mobile architects form enclavic networks with other mobile architects, engineers and similar people with a cosmopolitan outlook. So these networks have a post-national character (Kennedy 2004, 176). As one architect in his study reported: 'Our friends are mostly people from across the world. They are people who travel both physically and mentally … people who don't find other cultures to be a problem' (Kennedy 2004, 175).

Such networks are, we can say, on the move. As people move from project team to project team, from city to city, the links and bridges within these networks multiply and expand across time–space. Since these people are rich in networking tools and master the art of keeping in touch, more and more people are enrolled into a revolving circuit of transnational social life. Kennedy sums up: 'Eventually, as friends move and form, or join, other networks with more likeminded individuals in the next host country, and because previous contacts are maintained, yet more friends are added to the revolving circuits of transnational social life' (2004, 176).

Ó Riain also researched transnational teamworking among global professionals (2000). This study shows how software developers from various countries rely upon intense face-to-face teamworking to meet tight project deadlines and search out new projects. These ad hoc project teams have much autonomy in arranging and performing their work so long as they meet the deadline: 'the politics of the contemporary workplace is increasingly the politics of time' executed through tight project deadlines (Ó Riain 2000, 178). To meet these deadlines these groups work together in a shared physical space and forge solidarity and an intense team spirit. However, once the project is finished, the group fragments and people use their networks to become part of a new project, locally or elsewhere.

Ó Riain's and Kennedy's studies show how the distinction between strong ties and weak ties is less marked for those with mobile lives. Weak ties can become strong when working in a project team and they become weak again when the project finishes, if they are not maintained over the distances now involved.

These studies also illustrate the 'liquid' nature of networking and networked sociality. Bauman stresses that the modern workplace has become a 'camping site' where no one stays for long before moving onto the next job (2000a, 149). Networks within workplaces are loosely tied; they are constantly untied and retied; people keep their distance at the same time as they relate: their networks work through instantaneity and disposability. In *Liquid Love* Bauman summarizes the logic of such individualized networking:

> Unlike 'relations', 'kinships', 'partnerships', and similar notions that make the mutual engagement while excluding or passing over in silence its opposite, the disengagement, 'network' stands for a matrix for simultaneous connecting and disconnecting ... In a network, connecting and disconnecting are equally legitimate choices, enjoy the same status and carry the same importance. (2003, xii)

As Florida's research also suggests, such people do not desire the strong ties, long-term commitments and spatial fixity characteristic of Putnam's social capital; they wish for fluid, diverse and mobile communities where one can plug in and out with great ease and easily build a wide range of relationships (2002, 220; and see Sennett 1999 on the resulting 'corrosion of character'). Bauman notes how the lack of trust involved here produces a corresponding significance of those: 'spaces reserved for face-to-face meetings ... [that] play a crucial role in the integration of that elite' (2003, 114).

Although this mobile, networked work is likely to become empirically more significant, it is not yet typical and anyway is constrained by other aspects, especially friendship, relationships and family life. Much mobility research has focused upon professionals with many weak ties but seemingly very few strong ones (for similar research see Beaverstock 2005; Kesselring 2006; Lassen 2006). In his ongoing research of 'knowledge industries' as 'transport-generating enterprises', Lassen claims that the work of scientists, engineers, architects, educators, writers, artists, entertainers as we all as many traditional businessmen is characterized by high levels of international mobility and of virtual communication (2006). However, in fact his study shows that the average Hewlett-Packard employee in Denmark only flies 3.8 times a year, while academics from Aalborg University, Denmark, fly only twice a year for academic purposes.

Thus some research here overemphasizes individualized networking and overlooks the relational commitments that people have to their social networks (Conradson and Latham 2005a). However, there are exceptions. Holmes's (2004) study of academics in relationships with partners living elsewhere indicates that many mobile professionals are constrained by their relationship and therefore partly 'directed' by their partner. It also shows that distant relationships can come at a high price; for many couples it is something they have to live with, for shorter or longer periods, if both of them work. An extensive survey in Germany suggests that for about one in three long-distance relationships mobility is a 'forced' choice

(Limmer 2004). Green and Canny's research shows that professionals are much more willing to relocate to pursue a career if they are single and do not have family responsibilities. If couples do relocate, there is a high probability that one person has to sacrifice his or (more likely) her career (2003). The phenomenon of 'trailing spouses' is a powerful illustration of this kind of dependent mobility (Cresswell 2001, 2002). We continue this discussion by reviewing some literature and research dealing with family life.

Networked Family Life

The modern family is said to be undergoing major transformations that we will briefly adumbrate. First, family life is becoming plugged into an ever-expanding array of communication technologies that connect families to one another and to the outside world. The typical modern family with two teenagers is said to have several landline phones, three or four mobile phones, a couple of computers, a number of cameras (including a digital one) and video cameras, perhaps four email accounts, at least one car and some travel cards. In addition there are TV sets, DVDs and videos, stereos, magazines and a newspaper as well as various credit cards. The family has become a communications hub: 'No longer a sanctuary where the family was relatively shielded from intrusions from the outside world, the home is now a communication hub, infused with messages of diverse and increasingly global origins' (Bachen 2001, 1). Yet these 'machines' also enable local ordering as the coordination of seemingly endless journeys to work, school, recreational and domestic activities that would be practically impossible without email, text messages, telephone calls and diaries. 'Families and technologies in households are inter-connected as elements of the same system' (Bachen 2001, 2). So there is a widespread adoption of mobility tools by ordinary families that afford the mobilization of social networks, with the making and sustaining of connections at-a-distance.

Second, there is a large increase in the sheer number of households, as each household shrinks in size. This is a global trend, with an annual growth rate in the number of households of 2.3 per cent between 1985 and 2000, while the world's population is growing by only 1.5 per cent per annum (Liu et al 2003). We might say that families are becoming more networked, becoming less nuclear so much as 'unclear' (Bauman 2003). It is claimed that the family is under siege, as signalled by growing divorce rates, single parenthood, joint custody, co-habitation, singles, stepfamilies and gay couples. In particular among couples without children, long-distance relationships are common, especially because women pursue careers more or less as men do (Walby 1997; Holmes 2004, 190). Many dual-career couples will at one point live apart. In Britain, in the late 1990s there were 157,000 divorces; if this trend continues, 40 per cent of all marriages will end in divorce. There are now in the UK 1.6 million lone parents. It is estimated that 7 per cent of all children live with a stepmother or stepfather. Most extended families involve one or more stepfamilies (Allan and Crow 2001, 25, 26, 34). 'Unclear' families are fragmented, not only socially but also spatially, with most families moving house after a divorce. Moving back and forth between one's mother's and father's new place of residence involves considerable travel for children and parents, especially if one of them relocates to another city or region (Allan and Crow 2001, 132).

Third, this high rate of household dissolution does not seem to undermine people's desire for family life. To live with another person on a stable basis and at some stage to have children is still seen as natural; the nuclear family is a powerful myth within the collective imagination. What is new is that splitting up and remarrying is also normal. So the remedy for the so-called crisis of the family is the family! People live in a frenzy of love, in what is called the 'normal chaos of love' (Beck and Beck-Gernsheim 1995). Giddens argues that the family is being recovered as a pure relationship in a democracy of contingent love (1992). It is the romantic complex of 'forever' and 'one-and-only' qualities with which Giddens contrasts his notions of 'pure relationships' and 'confluent love'. 'Pure love' is lived out in impure families. Such relationships exist because of love, and if they do not deliver emotional satisfaction, they break up:

> The general diagnosis is that people's lives are becoming more mobile, more porous, and of course more fragile. In the place of pre-given and often compulsory types of relationship is appearing 'until the next thing' principle, as Bauman calls it, a kind of refusal of lifelong plans, permanent ties, immutable identities ... Instead of fixed forms, more individual choices, more beginnings and farewells. (Beck-Gernsheim 2002, 123)

Thus it is said that the family is becoming individualized, part of a wider individualization of 'reflexive modern societies'.

However, some researchers contest this individualized version of family life, partly because it can be apocalyptic: 'One can, it seems, begin to predict the growth of societies where kinship networks cease to exist, where few couples will commit to each other beyond a few years, where children who have experienced their parents' divorce become deeply ambivalent about marriage, and where there is almost frenetic emotional mobility and only fleeting, serial relationships' (Smart and Shipman 2004, 493). Mason argues that the 'individual, reflexive author' is the reality of only 'a highly privileged minority of white middle class men, apparently unencumbered by kinship or other interpersonal commitments' (2004b, 163). The 'individualization thesis' is said to overlook how commitments and obligations continue within families and keep them 'tied together', not least when (small) children are involved. In her study of personal narratives about residential histories in the North-West of England, Mason shows that social identity and agency are relational rather than individualized concepts:

> When the people in our study talked about where they had lived and why, they talked about relationships with other people, especially family and kin, but also friends, neighbours and sometimes colleagues and workmates. Indeed their discussions of context, contingency, constraint and opportunity were themselves highly relational in that they were grounded

in and spoke of changing webs of relationship and connection rather than any kind of strategic individualism or motivation. (2004a, 166–7)

Similar relational narratives are to be found in Hammerton's study of how the post-war generation of British working-class immigrants to Canada and Australia constructed their immigration and family stories (2004). The stories told by these people are partly recollections of the pain and guilt of leaving people behind, of separating families. Given that money was scarce, long-distance travelling high-priced, and communication slow and costly, these migrants lost contact with family and friends back home. While they came to experience relative financial and professional success, their 'homesickness' almost ruined it (2004, 274).

Moreover, modern families in the UK are often comprised of migrants and mixed-race families. The number of international migrants worldwide doubled between 1960 and 2000 (UNDP 2004, 87). The migration literature shows that migration is rarely an isolated decision pursued by individual agents but rather a collective action involving families, kinships and other communal contacts. Migrants travel to join established groups of settlers who provide transnational arrangements for them in receiving countries, while simultaneously retaining links with their country of origin and with chains of other immigrants (Goulborne 1999; Salaff, Fong and Siu-Lin 1999; Ryan 2004, 355).

So migration disperses family members and friends across vast areas and thus the intimate networks of care, support and affection – effectively social capital – stretch over large geographical distances (Chamberlain 1995). Scholars of kinship and migration have long known that presence and absence – or proximity and distance – do not necessarily conflict. Thus 'geographical proximity or distance do not correlate straightforwardly with how emotionally close relatives feel to one another, nor indeed how far relatives will provide support or care for each other' (Mason 2004a, 421; see also Mason 1999). Indeed intimacy and caring can take place at-a-distance, through letters, packets, photographs, emails, money transactions, telephone calls and recurrent visits. So, caring, obligations and indeed presence do not necessarily imply co-presence or face-to-face proximity: people can be near, in touch and together, even when great distances tear them physically apart. As Callon and Law maintain more generally, 'presence is not reducible to co-presence ... co-presence is both a location and a relation' (2004, 6, 9).

These various studies show that most people's biographies and mobilities are relational, connected and embedded rather than individualized. They are, though, individualized in the sense that each person's networks and relations are specific to that individual (see above). People are enmeshed in social dramas that have social and emotional consequences. Networks both enable and constrain possible 'individual' actions. This is the case not only for people in relationships and families but also for 'singles' that increasingly form tight-knit groups of friends where care and support flourish, according to Watters in *Urban Tribes* (2004; see also Weston 1991, as well as much of the research reported below).

Conclusion

In this chapter we examined various ways of analysing social networks in the modern world. We reviewed the social capital, social network and small worlds approaches. We then outlined a mobilities approach to such topics. We went on to examine some studies – mainly in the UK – that reveal the importance of social networks within work and family life. Such networks vary significantly, depending in part upon people's travelling and communications practices that sustain the weak and strong ties within *and* across networks. We also saw that more or less all networks depend upon intermittent meetings involving travel and communications by some or all participants. Meetings central to networks can be costly in terms of time, money and effort, as we explore in detail in the next chapter.

Chapter 3

Meetings and Networks

Introduction

In this chapter we consider the social science literature on meetings, an undeveloped field but one essential for deciphering the nature of networks and travel. First, we demonstrate the wide array, scale and organizational importance of face-to-face meetings within many kinds of work environment. Second, we show how such meetings are significantly about establishing and maintaining networks. Third, we consider the possibilities of substituting various kinds of communicative and virtual encounters for physical meetings. We argue that there are some possibilities of substitution here but still many things are achieved within co-present meetings mean that they are here to stay for a good time yet; and hence physical travel is also here to stay. Finally, we turn the issue around and consider how leisure travel and tourism seem increasingly about co-present meetings and less about purely travelling to view the exotic. Thus we show the importance of meetings taking place within families, especially of migrants and diasporas, and that a significant amount of tourist-type travel is really as much about sociability as a search for exotic places. Overall, we show how tourist-type travel is important within mobile, networked societies.

It should be noted that we mainly deal here with the literature relating to business-type meetings although our research more concerns meetings with friends and families. We deal with business-type meetings since that is where useful literature has been most developed.

'Business of Talk'

The scale of business meetings is enormous. Even back in 1988, the USA's major 500 companies were said to have held between 11 and 15 million formal meetings each day and 3–4 billion meetings each year. Managers spend up to half of their time in such face-to-face meetings and much of their time involves working with and evaluating colleagues through long and intense periods of physical co-presence and talk. The typical day of top executives consists almost exclusively of planning meetings, attending meetings and executing the decisions made at meetings. Talk face-to-face and on the phone can occupy 75 per cent of an executive's time (Boden 1994, 51; Boden and Molotch 1994, 272; Romano and Nunamaker 2001, 4). Strassmann summarizes: 'there are meetings, and meetings about meetings, and meetings to plan reports, and meetings to review the status of reports. And what these meetings are about is people just trying to figure out what they are doing' (cited in Romano and Nunamaker 2001, 4). Moreover, the ubiquitous meeting tool, 'the personal diary', makes sure that a new meeting is arranged, as the present meeting is coming to an end:

> One of the unstated protocols of modern work is that those attending meetings should bring their diaries and schedule into their future the circle of forthcoming meetings. Indeed, this forms part of the ritualistic end of meeting: the entry into the diary of the next meeting. Indeed, the notion 'diarize' has been coined to describe this ritual. (Symes 1999, 373)

Schwartzman (1989) understands meetings as communicative events with specific norms of speaking and interacting, oratorical genres and styles, interest and participation. The commonsense notion of what meetings are and do in organizations is mistaken since:

> Instead of accepting task-focused assumptions that suggest that decisions, crises, conflicts, and the like are what meetings are about, the opposite is proposed here, that is, that meetings are what decisions, problems, and crisis are about. Meetings reproduce themselves by the volume of decisions, crises and the like that an organisation produces. (Schwartzman 1989, 9–10)

In other words, decisions, problems, and crises occur because they produce meetings and meetings produce organizations, and not the other way round. So organizations are about meetings, organizations are made and remade through the performances of meetings (Schwartzman 1989, 40–1, 86). Schwartzman defines a meeting as:

> a gathering of three or more people who agree to assemble for a purpose ostensibly related to the functioning of an organisation or group. The event is characterised by multiparty talk that is episodic in nature, and participants either develop or use specific conventions for regulating this talk. (1989, 63)

Important aspects here are the physical coordination and assembling of at least three people at the same place, their roles and their speech performances. Schwartzman distinguishes between two types of meetings according to 'time, formality and representation': scheduled and unscheduled meetings. Scheduled meetings are pre-arranged, scheduled for a specific time and place, having an explicit agenda, perhaps materialized as a paper document, with more or less formal turn-taking and minutes. By contrast, unplanned meeting talk is loosely regulated and informal in conversational style and there is seldom a need to report back. Unplanned meetings often involve bumping-into-each encounters and especially 'knock-on-the-door' meetings when problems and enquiries have to be solved immediately face-to-face.

Drawing in part upon Schwartzman, Boden sees organizations as a human accomplishment of face-to-face conversation: people in organizations do work by arranging meetings, attending them and talking at them. Meetings constitute organizations because 'meetings are, by their very nature talk. Talk, talk, talk and more talk' (Boden 1994, 8, 82). Meetings are 'ritual affairs, tribal gatherings in which the faithful reaffirm solidarity and warring factions engage in verbal battles … When in doubt call a meeting. When one meeting isn't enough, schedule another' (Boden 1994, 81).

Talk is made up of sets of utterances that carry out tasks or do things. Such performative utterances include making contacts, forming trust, doing deals, repairing connections, networking, agreeing contracts and celebrating achievements. A co-present meeting is often necessary to talk through problems and make major decisions. Conversations are produced, topics can come and go, misunderstandings can be quickly corrected and commitment and sincerity can be directly assessed. Trust between people is thus something that gets worked at, involving a joint performance by those in such conversations. Conversations are made up of not only words, but expressions that indicate various meanings, facial gestures, body language, status, voice intonation, pregnant silences, past histories, anticipated conversations and actions, turn-taking practices and so on.

Turn taking is highly structured. The ebb and flow of talk is a simple but highly effective system. Turn taking works 'like a revolving gate, demanding and facilitating deft entry and exist, and effectively managing the flow of talk by spacing speakers and pacing topics' (Boden 1994, 66). Turns are valued, distributed between participants and normally involving one speaker talking at any time. Turns are not allocated in advance, turn transition is quick and there are few gaps and overlaps in turn transition.

The embodied character of conversation is thus: 'a managed physical action as well as "brain work"' (Boden and Molotch 1994, 262). 'It is this richness of information', Boden argues, that make us feel that we need co-presence to know what is really going on, including the degree to which others are providing us with reliable, reasonable accounts (Boden and Molotch 1994, 259). Compared with co-present conversations, letters, memos, faxes and email seem less effective at establishing and sustaining such long-term trust relations (Boden and Molotch 1994, 263–7).

This thus means that even in virtual economies and organizations physical meeting-places are necessary for trustful relationships. Boden summarizes how in fast moving financial services:

> Surrounded by complex technology and variable degrees of uncertainty, social actors seek each other out, to make the deals that, writ large across the global electronic boards of the exchanges, make the market. They come together in tight social worlds to use each other and their shared understanding of 'what's happening' to reach out and move those levers that move the world. (2000, 194)

So a powerful 'compulsion to proximity' ensures that face-to-face meetings flourish within the business context (and by implication within many other social domains). They are also said to be superior in sparking creative ideas:

All the technologies in the world do not – at least yet, and maybe never – replace face-to-face contact when it comes to brainstorming, inspiring passion, or enabling many kinds of serendipitous discovery ... Fax is fine one-way communication, e-mail for two-way asynchronous and relatively emotionless communication; telephone and communications that require no visual aids; and video conferencing if no subtlety in body language is necessary. But face-to-face communication is the richest multi-channel medium because it enables use of all the senses, is interactive and immediate. (Leonard and Swap cited in Thrift 2000, 684–5; see Bauman 2003)

It is interesting that this romanticized view of face-to-face meetings is at odds with anecdotes within popular media and management books where meetings are portrayed as boring and wasteful. In one study 'corporate vice presidents admitted to falling asleep or dozing away off during a meeting presentation and they reported that they found more than forty-three percent of business meetings boring' (Romano and Nunamaker 2001, 9). While some meetings take place in new and interesting places, it appears that many meetings are dull and repetitive, especially internal staff meetings.

With the exception of most internal staff meetings, meetings almost always involve travel by some or all participants, with many conferences, symposia, bonding events, camps and so on being located on 'neutral territory'. Often travel to and from a meeting will be more time consuming than the actual meeting. In Norway, job-related meetings account for about 60 per cent of all (domestic and international) flights (Høyer and Ness 2001), while the figure is 40 per cent in Denmark (Lassen 2006). Meetings and related travel are the third-largest discretionary expense after salaries and data processing for businesses (Collis 2000). Since travel is crucial for performing business life, it cannot be easily avoided. Or as an American Express Consulting Manager says: 'A business that needs people to travel so they can generate revenue can't afford to cut out travel' (cited in Davidson and Cope 2003, 34). Therefore, even in times of economic recession and perceived dangers of travelling, the scale of the conference industry is said to be fairly stable:

> One of the positive characteristics of the conference industry is its resilience, even in times of economic downturn. While there may be a trading down, many events still go ahead: public companies are required to hold an Annual General meeting for their shareholders, senior managers need to engage in management retreats to explore ways of reviving their business, new products are launched, staff still have to be trained and motivated, sales forces need to be brought together for briefings, and many other types of conference take place, albeit with reduced budgets. (Rogers cited in Davidson and Cope 2003, 13)

Davidson and Cope's examination of conferences, conventions, incentive travel and corporate hospitality bring out how business trips often have touristic qualities, and therefore how business travel and tourism can and often will overlap (2003; see also Weber and Chan 2003, and the final section of this chapter). 'Indeed for some forms of business travel, the leisure and pleasure element is absolutely crucial to the reason for making the trip in the first place: incentive trips that are composed almost entirely of leisure, recreational and cultural pursuits, only achieve their objectives if participants thoroughly enjoy themselves' (Davidson and Cope 2003, 256).

Even normal business trips occasionally become touristic when they expand into weekend breaks, which were particularly common with airlines' 'Saturday Night Rule' (Davidson and Cope 2003, 257). According to Høyer and Ness, academic conferences are being organized in new and ever-more exotic places and they suggest how conferencing functions as a form of conspicuous consumption through which power is displayed, networks are sustained and interesting places are toured (2001). For instance, the 'delegates attending TIAFT 2000, the Helsinki-based conference of the International Association of Forensic Toxicologists, chose from a number of post-conference tours including a three-day Lapland Arctic Safari, a one-day cruise to Tallinn, Estonia, and a three-day trip to St Petersburg by train' (Davidson and Cope 2003, 254). As Collis argues, most (long-distance) meetings have an incentive, or leisurely aspect (2000, 2). Davidson and Cope suggest that the touristic nature of conferences is what keeps them alive:

> perhaps the strongest argument against conferences being in danger of being replaced by Internet or videoconferencing technology is the very simple one …: 'Delegates enjoy them!' – not only for the opportunities they provide to update knowledge and network with like-minded people, but also due to the fact that they are often located in cities of tourist interest, and offer other peripheral pleasures such as the social programme, the partners programme and the type of pre- and post-conference. (2003, 139)

However, while many business trips have become touristic, a counter tendency is that today's business traveller can find it more difficult to escape the office. No longer is the person in transit also *incommunicado* (Ling and Yttri 1999). Now that laptops, PDAs, blackberries, communicators and mobile phones are standard equipment among business people, and as airports, hotels, cafés, planes and trains are increasingly designed as workspaces with internet and laptop connections, business travellers have fewer opportunities for a disconnected rest or a touristic stroll. Places-in-transit become 'a high-tech command centre' from which business people communicate with clients and colleagues. It is expected of business travellers that the office can reach them in real time and that they respond to phone calls, text messages, emails, faxes and so on. 'Taking off on a business trip used to mean getting away from it all. But corporate downsizing and new information technology (which both allow and require you to be totally wired at all times) have forced travellers to be more accountable and productive when they're away' (Collis 2000, 112; Lyons and Urry 2005). Mobile communication systems and 'personalized networking' are doubled-edged swords that simultaneously allow contact with absent others as well as monitoring by absent others. They allow 'for a sense of presence at a distance that allows the traveller to be always available, and therefore always under surveillances' (Molz 2006). As Urry says:

> To inhabit such machines is to be connected to, or to be at home with, 'sites' across the world – while simultaneously such sites can monitor, observe, and trace each inhabited

machine ... others being uncannily present *and* absent, here and there, near and distant, home and away, proximate and distant. (2004a, 35)

Meetings and Networking

Some commentators argue that face-to-face meetings and conferences are being transformed since information can travel the world in seconds. Weber and Chan state that: 'Since more information can now be exchanged via technology, there is a greater need to build relationships when getting together for face-to-face meetings. Consequently, meetings in the future will focus more on social aspects rather than on business, which may be conducted mainly via technology' (2003, 206). Face-to-face interactions appear to be less concerned with traditional (one-way) presentations of information and passive listening and more with building and sustaining networks and exchanging social goods. Future business meetings, it is said, will be active and participatory in style, involving networking, two-way communication, hands-on experiences and workgroups (Davidson and Cope 2003, 139).

Lodge's novel *Small World* reveals this complex, multilayered and richly gossipy nature of conferences and by implication many other 'occasioned meetings'. He describes such conferences: 'you journey to new and interesting places, meet new and interesting people, and form new and interesting relationships with them; exchange gossip and confidences ...; eat, drink and make merry in their company every evening; and yet ... return home with an enhanced seriousness of mind' (1985, 1). *Small World* brings out that what gets exchanged in such conferences through intense and dynamic conversational interactions are rich social goods. These include friendship, power, projects, markets, information, rumours, job deals, sexual favours, gossip and trust. Conferences are full of small world experiences as apparent strangers discover they are connected through weak ties. In a similar fashion, Collis proclaims that in real meetings:

> The social drink, the impromptu meeting, can be pure gold. It is nothing you can quantify; it's intuitive; gut-feel; keeping faith with serendipity. Who, for example, goes to a conference to listen to the presentations? It's networking that counts. Or the chance to bond with your boss or other colleagues for an extended time. (2000, 64)

Mintzberg calls this the ritualistic phase of meetings:

> Gossip about peers in the industry is exchanged; comments are made on encounters the participants have recently had or on published material they have recently read; important political events are discussed and background information is traded. It seems reasonable to conclude that the manager collects much information in these discussions, and that this fact makes the formal, face-to-face meeting a powerful medium. (cited in Schwartzman 1989, 75)

The social productiveness of meetings as networking and trust-generating is also clear in Nandhakumar's ethnographic study of virtual teams operating on a global scale. As a manager of a virtual team says:

> We are having a global team meeting in two weeks time ... the big joke is – 'can't you do this virtually?'... I say no we can't do it virtually, we can get so far virtually but before we have a real good drink and a good meal and a good social chat at length we are not going to be a 'real team' ... We can then use technology to maintain it. (cited in Nandhakumar 1999, 53)

Echoing Boden, this study suggests that personalized trust relationships are essential for virtual teamworking, and while personalized trust relationships can be to some degree sustained virtually, face-to-face interactions and socialization are required to establish trust in the first place (Nandhakumar 1999, 55).

Another example of how virtual teams depend upon face-to-face meetings is seen in Brown and O'Hara's (2003) research on mobile workers. The main reason why these workers are on the move is to meet people face-to-face. However, their meetings are far from formal and scheduled – accidental encounters with colleagues 'on the road' and back at the office are important for workers that spend most of their day without face-to-face exchanges of information, gossip and sociality:

> The motivation of the mobile workers is to put themselves in a position that would increase the likelihood of 'bumping into' their co-workers. This networking was seen as their 'bread and butter' in terms of their long-term development of knowledge, which they could bring to bear on both current and future work situations. (Brown and O'Hara 2003, 1573–4)

Networking and showing one's face seem important in business meetings especially to those in the knowledge industries. The ideal spaces of such multifaceted networking are places with a cultural buzz. Workplaces move away from the formal office occupied for work nine–five, to a 'club' full of informal conversation, brainstorming and gossip (Cairncross 1997, 41). Indeed new office buildings are increasingly designed around 'club space' that is more for meeting up on those intermittent days of co-presence (Thrift 2000; Laurier, Whyte and Buckner 2001). Such business is moving back into the café scene 200 years after Lloyds Insurance of London began in a coffee house and only later acquired its own office buildings. Starbucks is playing a major role in this development with 4,500 cafés in the USA and 1,500 across Europe. Laurier, Whyte and Buckner analyse how stylized cafés are 'busy meeting grounds' where business people meet up and hang out with workmates and conduct informal meetings with clients and business partners (2001).

Wittel's research noted above discusses how cities such as London and New York have a broad range of networking events and places in which new media workers intermittently catch up, socially and professionally, through quick exchanges of information and sociality (2001). In such networking places some distinctions between social life and professional life, friends, workmates and clients are blurred.

There is a proliferation of urban places of cool, creative sociality and community where social networks do business and have fun while consuming good coffee and drink. Crucially, such face-to-face sociality and meeting-places make small worlds of expressive sociality in otherwise impersonal 'big worlds':

> I mean the beautiful thing about New York is that a lot of people know each other, help each other, introduce each other, network ultimately. And you can't, a lot of people when they don't see each other at these kinds of events, forget you. New York is small but at the same time it's very big as well. You live in the same area, you don't meet each other all the time, so you somehow lose contact. So these meetings and these conferences for me are about being seen and seeing other people again, saying hello being sort of on the back of their mind and it's usually like a two-minute conversation like how are you doing, how is your business and that is all it needs. (cited in Wittel 2001, 67)

Indeed, research on new media professionals and the 'creative class' suggest that a city's economic power and ability to attract investment and creative (new media) professionals rest upon whether they have a vibrant, tolerant and inclusive cultural scene where people can network, easily meet new people and bump into like-minded people in small-world ways and yet live independent lives (Florida 2002; Pratt 2002). As cities are increasingly expected to have 'buzz', to be creative, and generally to bring forth powers of invention and intuition, so the active engineering of the affective register of cities is developed. Cities must exhibit intense expressiveness to attract creative people, who in turn attract innovative companies. Florida's studies show that the economic power of a city depends upon its cultural capital, that is, their tolerance, inclusiveness and cultural buzziness. Cities with a vibrant cultural scene, high mobility and dense concentrations of immigrants, gays and bohemian people are best at attracting the 'creative class' that in turn attracts capital; companies, it is said, follow people and not the other way round (Florida 2002; Thrift 2004, 58).

Virtual Meetings

In this section we consider whether and to what degree virtual 'meetings' can substitute for physical co-presence, still mainly using business-oriented literature (this is also considered in the next chapter in a somewhat different way). We cannot ignore communication technologies and portray communication purely as a sequence of face-to-face-encounters within specific fixed physical spaces. 'As many HP [Hewlett-Packard] virtual team members work at home, or on the road, mobile technologies such as cell phones and wireless networks make it possible to conduct virtual meetings from (almost) anywhere, anytime' (Jones, Oyung and Pace 2002).

Rather differently, Hiller and Franz discuss how diasporic websites are important 'meeting-places' to gain 'new ties', sustain 'old ties' and recuperate 'lost ties':

> The Newfoundland Kitchen has always been a meeting place for family and friends to exchange thoughts and news, the center of any social event, sing-a-long or party. We would like for you to use the kitchen to meet new friends and keep in touch with old

friends, thank people for acts of kindness, wish them a happy birthday or anniversary ... So come on in, help yourself to a cup of tea, pull up a chair and enjoy the company. (2004, 742)

First then, with the unprecedented diffusion of mobile phones social scientists have begun to take telecommunications seriously (Katz and Aakhus 2002a, 2002b; Licoppe 2004). Research shows that the greater the geographical distance between people, the longer they talk, when they do talk (see Licoppe 2004). Immigrants, people with family members abroad and long-distance couples frequently engage in lengthy and recurrent telephone conversations; (transnational) connectivity through cheap telephone calls is at the heart of their lives (Holmes 2004; Pribilsky 2004; Vertovec 2004). Long-distance calls seem to resemble physical meetings: they are lengthy turn-taking encounters through which gossip is shared, troubles are talked through, previous meetings are evaluated, solidarity is expressed, roles affirmed and future meetings arranged. They are the best substitute for physical meetings when these cannot take place.

Future landline telephone meetings are likely to be more meeting-like as information and communication technologies enables 'audio conferences' that can involve everything from three or four family members to hundreds of business people. Microsoft's program NetMeeting allow such 'internet telephony gatherings' for free (if broadbanded), no matter where one's friends or family members happen to be.

At British Telecom (BT) itself, teleconferencing is used by 92 per cent of all staff and half of these participate five or more times per month. BT's 108,000 staff made 350,000 audio conference calls in 2003. The majority of these meetings last up to an hour and typically involve six to seven participants. Over half of relevant BT staff are certain that their last teleconference replaced a face-to-face meeting, while only 5 per cent said that it helped in scheduling a future face-to-face meeting. Thus BT conducted thousands of 'meetings' without any associated journeys. In terms of petrol alone, the cost saved by BT is around £6 million a year. More generally, most companies that promote teleconferencing report reductions of between 10 and 30 per cent in overall travel expenses (Cairns et al 2004, 293–5).

Indeed, Boden's positive view of face-to-face interaction and eye contact overlooks how the visual sense can reduce trust and engender superficial encounters relying on outward signs. This issue is interestingly addressed within an internal Hewlett-Packard article:

However, there are situations where virtual meetings are preferable (for reasons above and beyond limiting travel). For example, it's more difficult to form first-impression stereotypes about someone in a virtual meeting. We recently received an e-mail from an HP employee confined to a wheelchair. The writer commented that meeting virtually is preferable for him because people can't form an impression of him based on his disability. (Jones, Oyung and Pace 2002)

The highlighting of bodily attraction and appearance in face-to-face meetings is replaced by textual and poetic adroitness in on-line meetings, and this can be an advantage for those whose physical appearance is not their best 'selling point' or, more positively put, that are interested in knowing 'whole people' rather than 'performances of appearance'. This may partly explain the apparent popularity of the internet for dating and texting (sending SMS messages), especially among young people. While text messages, emails and cyberspaces can be seen as impoverished media for the presentation of the self because of their reduced communication cues, they afford new opportunities for self-disclosure, control or flirting:

> Text messaging [and emails] may be one strategy for teenagers [and everybody else!] to present their more courageous selves. The corporeal presentation of the self has been filtered out, and the communicative device enables more control over the presentation of the self and message content. A less than successful attempt at this type of communication can easily be passed over referring to the playful quality of text messages, thus, to employ the Goffmanian term, elegantly withdrawing from the stage. (Oksman and Turtiainen 2004, 326; see also Henderson and Gilding 2004)

However, this provides a one-sided account, stressing the 'positive' elements of this sort of courageous interaction where people more or less secretly can play with identities. There are hugely problematic aspects to this virtual presentation of the self, with widespread public concerns about grooming of young teenagers by mature (potentially paedophile) adults; bullying in schools by text messaging; and offensive junk emails with offensive sexual content and so on. Almost half of the American internet users complain about unwanted junk emails (Kibby 2005, 770).

Another form of virtual meeting format is data conferencing. Data conferencing enables students, colleagues, collaborators and clients to exchange information digitally and work upon presentations, documents, texts, graphs and images in real time without rubbing shoulders. Data conferencing through NetMeeting is reported to be widely used at HP (Jones, Oyung and Pace 2002), while used by only 13 per cent of BT's staff (Cairns et al 2004, 290).

Videoconferencing allows facial appearance and 'facework' and most resembles face-to-face meetings (especially with advanced grid networks – AGNs). While videoconferences do substitute some face-to-face meetings and physical travel, an *Economist* article concludes that while they: 'are often seen as a cheaper alternative to travel, they are better understood as ... middle ground between a phone call and a face-to-face meeting ... videoconferencing is a perfect second tool after the first handshake' (Standage 2004). Along similar lines, Collis argues that 'videoconferencing is less about saving money on travel and more about global team working. It enables people to be brought into meetings who might not normally attend if they had to travel' (2000, 68).

So far videoconferencing is a thinner version of physical meeting in terms of bodily idiom and sociality. One cannot sense much of the client's office space, shake their hand, have sustained eye contact, observe all bodily expressions, taste their coffee, access their generosity, or finalize a deal over dinner overlooking the

Manhattan skyline. It is, in other words, a weaker medium to get to know someone. So videoconferences are not *yet* like face-to-face meetings.

Thus while virtual conferences will substitute for some face-to-face business travel it seems more likely that virtual meetings will be used to *supplement* traditional meetings, lectures, plenary sessions and conferences (Cairns et al 2004, 290). Moreover, face-to-face and virtual encounters are not separate worlds. Thus while participants meet in a disembodied virtual space, virtual meetings are real experiences taking place in physical locations; participants sip coffee, try to make themselves comfy in the chair, get nervous, excited and bored and so and so (on 'real' experiences in cyberspace, see Miller and Slater 2000).

Further, mobile technology also affects the way that people interact when face-to-face. Whereas Boden (1994) highlights differences between co-presence and communications, others show how they increasingly intermingle. Thus unmediated body-to-body talk is dwindling in modern societies that are saturated with machines, images and communication devices (Fortunati 2005). People are increasingly 'face-to-face-to-mobile-phone' as the mobile phone is brought along even when people meet socially (Katz and Aakhus 2002b: 2). Plant indeed notes how:

> Several Birmingham entrepreneurs say they use their mobiles as means of deliberately absenting themselves from their present environments and so keeping other people at bay: 'If I arrive at a meeting where I don't know anyone, I play for time and composure by doing things with my mobile'. This sends out other messages to the room as well: it says that one is busy and not to be disturbed, and temporarily extends one's personal space. (2000, 62)

Face-to-face meetings transform into face-to-interface interactions when computer documents are worked upon, PowerPoint presentations begin, mobile phones ring and so on. Face-to-face meetings are mediated and always connected to other meetings; they are typified by 'absent presence' (Gergen 2002). As Wittel says:

> it is impossible to separate face-to-face interactions from interactions over distance. In urban spaces the idea of an uninterrupted face-to-face sociality, disentangled from technological devices, is becoming a myth. More and more, we are experiencing an integration of long-distance communication in our realms of face-to-face interaction … It is hard to imagine a dinner of, let's say, four businessmen without a mobile ringing. (2001, 70)

We may thus say that face-to-face meetings are not any longer just face-to-face; they are partly becoming virtual meetings. As Callon and Law maintain more generally, 'presence is not reducible to copresence … copresence is both a location and a relation' (2004, 6, 9). Communications are now rarely a sequence of purely face-to-face-encounters within specific physical spaces (Katz and Aakhus 2002b; Licoppe 2004; Ling 2004).

Mobile phone cultures generate small worlds of perpetual catching up and small talk on the move, blurring distinctions between presence and absence. An extensive Cellnet-funded study by the Social Issues Research Centre suggests mobile phoning and texting are about networked gossiping, 'anytime, anyplace, anywhere', of living in 'connected presence' with one's more or less dispersed social networks (Fox 2001). Perpetual gossip at-a-distance helps people to come to terms with living in fast-paced and fragmented worlds where people less often physically bump into each other. Overall Fox argues that:

> We no longer live in the kind of small, close-knit tribes or communities ... where we would naturally be in daily contact with the members of our social network ... Most of us no longer enjoy the cosiness of a gossip over the garden fence. We may not even know our neighbours' names, and communication is often limited to a brief, slightly embarrassed nod, if that. Families and friends are scattered ... We are constantly on the move, spending much of our time commuting to and from work either among strangers on trains and buses, or alone and isolated in our cars ... [before the mobile phone] there was no telephonic equivalent of the regular brief and breezy encounters in a village or small community, where frequent passing exchanges – such as: 'Hello, nice day isn't it?', 'Yes, lovely – oh, how's your Mum?', 'Much better, thanks', 'Oh good – see you later then' – ensured that everyone felt connected to their social and support network ... Mobile phones are re-creating the more natural, humane communication patterns of pre-industrial times: we are using space-age technology to return to stone-age gossip. (2001)

So, widespread mobile phone ownership enables individualized yet connected small worlds of communication, in the midst of vast complex worlds of absence, distance and disconnection. Even when people are absent they can remain in communicative propinquity with their social networks, of work, family and friendship.

De-exoticizing Travel

In the next chapter we see how in the last decade or so there have been striking increases in business travel, tourist travel and migration, and in communications at-a-distance. The rich societies of the West and North have experienced 'time–space compression' as people travel to and connect with absent others faster, more conveniently and more cheaply than before (Harvey 1989).

This section shows that studies of tourism are relevant here because travel, visits and hospitality have moved centre-stage to many people's lives. The practices and meanings of tourist travel multiply and migrate into other aspects of mobility and social life – through business travel, migration, family life and friendship. Much travel is increasingly concerned with (re)producing social relations – with giving and receiving the hospitality of close friends, workmates and family members living elsewhere and fulfilling social obligations through attending Christmas parties, birthdays, weddings, funerals and so on (see also Larsen, Urry and Axhausen forthcoming). As Williams and Kaltenborn suggest: 'When we think of tourism we often think of travel to exotic destinations, but modernization has also dispersed and extended our network of relatives, friends and acquaintances' (1999, 214).

Statistical data partly documents this changing significance of travel to visit friends and relatives. World Tourism Organization statistics show that in 2001 there were 154 million international arrivals for 'VFR [visiting friends and relatives] health, religion, other', compared with 74 million in 1990. The average annual growth of 'VFR tourism' has been 8.5 per cent. In the same period trips undertaken for 'leisure, recreation and holidays' only increased by 4.2 per cent per year. In 1990 there were five times more 'leisure, recreation and holidays' travellers than 'VFR, health, religion, other' travellers; by 2001 this had reduced to little more than twice as many (http://www.world-tourism.org/facts/trends/purpose.htm; see also Seaton and Palmer 1997).

The turn to what we can call 'social' travel is also seen in recent international tourist arrivals to the UK. While holiday visits to the UK fell by 1.8 million to 8 million between 1999 and 2003, visits to friends or relatives increased by 1.3 million to 7 million. Thus when asked through a pre-coded questionnaire in which journeys can only have one specified purpose, almost as many international visitors state that they visit the UK to see their daughter or best friend as to visit Big Ben or the Lake District (National Statistics 2004). Connections at-a-distance have thus become widespread and tourist travel to meet with significant others is more feasible as many places are within reach quickly and cheaply by car and budget airline.

Therefore, much leisure travel should not be seen as marginal, superfluous and by implication unnecessary. Rather, travelling, visiting and hosting are necessary to much social life conducted at-a-distance. We take tourist travel to refer to all kind of non-work related physical travel that results in at least one overnight stay away from home, but for no more than a year. Tourist travel thus takes many cultural and organizational forms and it comprises both traditional journeys to extraordinary places and visits to significant others, hotels and private homes, and they will sometimes overlap in practice. Future travel surveys and tourist typologies need to be more sophisticated in their categories in order to capture how many journeys serve several purposes and combine various mode of travel, as when meetings or conferences are followed up by a weekend break, or migrants return home, or migrants receive guests from back home and so on. The term 'VFR tourism' is also unsatisfactory because it underemphasizes the significances of visiting place, as if VFR tourism exclusively involves social travel without regard to location.

Much early tourism theory defined the nature of tourism through some rather fixed dualisms: leisure as opposed to work, away as opposed to home, authenticity as opposed to inauthenticity, the extraordinary as opposed to the ordinary, and guest as opposed to host (Cohen 1972; MacCannell 1976; Smith 1978; Urry 1990/2002). These distinctions identified worthwhile places or moments of the 'tourist gaze' (Urry 1990/2002). The tourism escape was portrayed as a special event (such as the annual summer holiday) taking place in contained places designed, regulated or preserved more or less specifically for tourism, such as resorts, sightseeing buses, hotels, attractions, paths, promenades and beaches. It was an escape from the ordinariness, commitments and alienation of home and a quest for more desirable and fulfilling places. Differences between tourists were explained in terms of the places they were attracted to and how they consumed them, visually or bodily, romantically or collectively, as high-cultural texts or liminal playgrounds or places where the active body comes to life (Urry 1995; the literature on pilgrimage is different in its emphases).

In MacCannell (1976) and Urry (1990/2002), the tourist is portrayed as a sight*seer*, visually consuming places through gazing, photographing and collecting sights. The tourist experience is narrowed down to one of 'facing' places. Veijola and Jokinnen (1994) were the first to suggest that this (male) visual paradigm overlooks the corporeality of tourism practices. Recently, however, male theorists – alongside women researchers such as Wearing and Wearing (1996), Johnston (2001) and Veijola and Jokinnen (2003) – have turned to ideas of embodiment and performance to destabilize the visual hegemony of images, cameras and gazes within tourism studies (Edensor 2000; Franklin and Crang 2001; Coleman and Crang 2002; Franklin 2003; Bærenholdt et al 2004). This literature demonstrates how *inter alia* backpackers, adventure tourists and families consume places by bodily immersion in the corporeal and cultural sense-scapes of local cultures, mountains and beaches. Whether tourist researchers research 'gazing or performing' (Perkins and Thorns 2001), they agree that tourist travel is about *place*. This is illustrated below:

> If places did not exist the tourism industry would have to invent them … Places are intrinsic for any kind of tourism. Without places to go to tourism would seem meaningless. Indeed most tourism theories have revolved around the central theme: why do people go to places other than home for sake of pleasure. (Bærenholdt et al 2004, 1)

However, this concentration upon place neglects issues of sociality especially with significant others as well as obligatory social events (but see Kaplan 1996; Wearing and Wearing 1996; Williams and Kaltenberg 1999; McCabe 2002). People have very strong obligations to family and friends. Of people surveyed in the UK, 70 per cent agreed that 'people should keep in contact with close family members even if they don't have much in common' (McGlone, Park and Roberts 1999, 152). There are social customs, obligations, and activities that substantial majorities identify as among the top necessities of life. These events include: celebrations on special occasions such as Christmas (83 per cent) and attending weddings and funerals (80 per cent), visits to friends or family (84 per cent), especially to those in hospital (Gordon et al 2000).

Fulfilling social obligations often requires physical co-presence, performing rituals and sustained quality time, often at a very particular moment. These obligations involve not only face-to-face talk but also sharing a well-prepared Christmas turkey, having an anniversary dinner, exchanging birthday gifts, sipping champagne on New Year's Eve, celebrating the Chinese New Year and so on. If these rituals do not take place at their right time, they cease to be meaningful. As Warde and Martens say about significant family meals: 'it is important to be present, if it is possible, because the meal symbolises a socially significant, temporally specific occasion. To have eaten the same meal the day before or the day after would not be a satisfactory substitute, even if many of the same people would be present' (2000, 217).

Telephone calls, text messages or courier-delivered flowers only substitute for a journey to, and physical presence at, a church, hospital or Christmas dinner, if people have a (very) good excuse for not being able to attend. Communications will often be too one-dimensional to fulfil significant social obligations.

Fulfilling social obligations required relatively little long-distance travel when walking and cycling were the major modes of travel and social networks were socially tightly knit and spatially dense. As discussed in Chapter 1, research shows that people now socialize less frequently with each other on a weekly basis, seemingly indicating a decline in social capital (McGlone Park and Roberts 1999; Putnam 2000). Yet these studies overlook how travel may counteract this. And when distant friends or family members do meet up, each visit may last longer. People compensate for the intermittence of meetings and the cost of transport (time, money and weariness) by spending a whole day or weekend or week(s) together, often staying in each other's homes. In other words, frequent yet short visits may turn into intermittent yet longer periods of face-to-face co-presence, of hosting and visiting. Obligations of visiting and showing hospitality become central to tourist travel and indeed social life at-a-distance, as cheaper and faster travel compress stretched-out networks. Given that mobility is integral to social life, then the social sciences can no longer equate closeness, ties and intensity of communion with geographical nearness and daily or weekly interactions. Tourist-type travel enters the lives of business people and global professionals, second-homeowners and their friends and families, exchange students and gap-year workers abroad, migrants and (former) refugees, people with distant friends and kin, and even otherwise immobile people with friends and families in distant places. Tourism is less the privilege of the rich few, but more something involving and affecting many people, as otherwise immobile people might occasionally visit or host distant kin or be heartbroken when they remain at-a-distance. Tourists indeed are no longer only found in hotels, sightseeing buses, museums, beaches and other places on the beaten track, but also within inner-city flats, suburban homes, local supermarkets and mundane places apparently off the beaten track (Franklin and Crang 2001).

Thus, recent work has begun to challenge tourism studies' traditional distinctions between home and away, the ordinary and the extraordinary, work and leisure, everyday life and holidays, by arguing that in transnational times tourist-type travel moves into less obviously touristic places. Franklin and Crang suggest that:

> Tourism is no longer a specialist consumer product or a mode of consumption: tourism has broken away from its beginning as a relatively minor and ephemeral ritual of modern life to become a significant modality through which transnational modern life is organised … it can no longer be bounded off as a discrete activity, contained tidily at specific locations and occurring during set aside periods. (2001, 7)

The notions of 'dwelling-in-travel' and 'travelling-in-dwelling' (Clifford 1997) deconstruct distinctions between home and away by pointing to the possibilities of being at home while travelling and coming home through travel. As Clifford argues: 'Once traveling is foregrounded as a cultural practice, then dwelling, too, needs to be reconceived – no longer simply the ground from which traveling departs and to which it returns' (1997, 44; see also Franklin and Crang 2001, 6). Kaplan describes how her family was scattered across the USA and other continents. Tourist travel was thus 'unavoidable, indisputable, and always necessary for family, love and friendship' (1996, ix). Through tourist travel she came to be at home at various places and face-to-face with loved ones. If household members are regularly on the move then the distinction of home and away loses its analytical power, and family life no longer typifies stasis. Now that home for many people is not *one* place but various locations, people often express the desire to stay connected with former places of home(s). Tourist travel, we may thus hypothesize, represents not just an escape from home but also a *search* for home(s).

Thus tourism visits are often essential to the lives of migrants, to diasporic cultures and generally to family life and friendship (Condon and Ogden 1996; Willams and Hall 2000; Coles and Timothy 2004). 'Many forms of migration', as Williams and Hall say, 'generate tourism flows, in particular through the geographical extension of friendship and kinship networks. Migrants may become poles of tourist flows, while they themselves become tourists in returning to visit friends and relations in their areas of origin' (2000, 7). O'Reilly shows how migration and tourism are complexly folded into each other in the case of British homeowners on Spain's Costa del Sol (2003; see also Gustafson 2002; Caletrio 2003). Retirement migration from northern Europe to tourist destinations in southern Europe generates much tourist travel. On average, retired immigrants receive seven visits a year from the UK and two out of three of these migrants 'return home' at least once a year (Williams et al 2000, 40–1). Such visits are clustered around Christmas, holiday periods and important family events (birthday, weddings, funerals and so on), indicating that they are tied into obligations of family life. It has also been documented how tourism is a major facilitator of subsequent migration (Oigenblick and Kirschenbaum 2002).

Migration is a far from one-way journey of leaving one's homeland behind, but often a two-way journey between two sets of 'homes' (Ahmed et al 2003; see also Baldassar 2001). 'The migration process appears to require a return, a journey back to the point of departure' (Goulborne 1999, 193). This is particularly the case with many migrants who are members of distinct diasporas. Diaspora entails the notion that 'the old country' where one is no longer living, exerts some claim upon one's identity and loyalty, and that there are desires and expectations to return there and to sustain networks. While diasporas traditionally involved a desire for permanent return, today's migrants can connect with their homeland through frequent virtual and imaginative travel and especially through occasional visits.

In Trinidad, for example, it is said that one can really only be a proper 'Trini' by going abroad and occasionally returning home to visit friends and kin. About 60 per cent of nuclear families are thought to have at least one family member living abroad (Miller and Slater 2000, 12, 36). Three-fifths of the journeys undertaken by Korean New Zealanders are to Korea, followed by journeys to Australia and Japan where many Korean New Zealanders have kin members (Kang and Page 2000, 57). Sutton's (2004) ethnography shows how cheaper, easier and faster travel have enabled large-scale family reunion parties amongst Afro-Caribbean migrants, assembling in one significant Caribbean place dispersed family members from various North Atlantic countries. At many gatherings, family members living abroad will outnumber Caribbean-based members. The numbers of participants in these events range from 50 to 250, indicating the massive transnational tourist travel that such events generate. Mason demonstrates how English people with Pakistani ancestors regularly visit Pakistan to be co-present with their kin, to keep their family networks alive (2004a). Young people in the Caribbean and Pakistani communities are especially encouraged by mothers and grandmothers to travel back to their villages of origin (Stephenson 2002; Mason 2004a).

The social obligations implicated within diasporic cultures are also often intricately intertwined with obligations to visit certain places, especially monuments, religious sites and places of cultural victory or loss. Each year more than 100,000 Israeli and American Jews visit former Nazi concentration camps in Poland (Ioannides and Ioannides 2004). Duval's research on return visits among Caribbean migrants provides examples of how parents of Caribbean origin feel obliged to keep in touch with their homeland and to introduce it personally to their children (2004a, 2004b).

Bærenholdt, Haldrup, Larsen and Urry also highlight that most tourists do not only bring their bodies but also their loved ones with them when they are on holiday (2004). Tourists not only encounter other bodies and places but also travel with significant others. Tourist places are valued for their ability to afford 'intimate proximities'. Thus, 'Tourists are not merely searching for authenticity of the Other. They also search the authenticity of, and between, themselves' (Wang 1999, 364). Holidays render the family members available and present to each other. They are together, not separated by work, commuting trips, schools, homework, leisure activities and so on. So it seems that families are most at home when away from home. Tourists consume places and thereby perform a special kind of togetherness. Families on holiday invest much work in staging and enacting happy social life – something especially shown through their performances for the camera (Larsen 2005; see also Haldrup and Larsen 2003). And we might note that having an argument with one's loved one(s) when on a holiday, at that moment when everything is supposed to be blissful, is especially stressful.

It also seems to be that much tourist travel even to typical tourist places is about visiting friends and family members. Kyle and Chick's (2004) ethnography of an American fair demonstrates how families repeatedly return to the fair because it has turned into a meeting-place where people maintain precious relationships with family members and friends living elsewhere. In similar fashion, Caletrio's study of Spanish tourists in Costa Blanca shows that many are repeat visitors who have established strong relationships with other regular visitors. For them, Costa Blanca is a 'familiar place' full of memories and meeting-places where dispersed social networks experience intense co-presence for some weeks or more each year (Caletrio 2003; see also Pons 2003).

Much tourist travel thus involves a particular combination of places and significant people; most tourists take a trip with significant others (unlike solitary business travellers) and they might visit or meet up with friends or kin. Few tourists thus see the world as a solitary *flâneur* without an intended destination and a social embeddedness. European people travel to see their parents in their old hometown or their migrated parents in Spain or their best friend now living in Sydney or an old university friend now lecturing in Moscow or their daughter studying in Beijing. So when people travel to friends or kin they simultaneously travel to particular places that are experienced through the host's social networks and accumulated knowledge of the cultural scene or of nature. Another way of expressing this is by saying that sociality matters in sightseeing and places matter in visiting friends and family. A further topic for research would be whether places seen through the 'eyes' of local 'hosting' residents are viewed differently from where places are encountered through 'impersonal' guidebooks and websites.

Conclusion

We have demonstrated the sheer scale and organizational importance of co-present meetings, and hence also of the travel that goes with them. Further, we showed that such meetings are significantly about establishing and maintaining networks, and indeed that places are increasingly about providing opportunities for meeting and networking. We also examined the possibilities of substituting various kinds of communications and virtual encounters for physical meetings. Overall we concluded that there are some possibilities here of substitution but many things get done within co-present meetings that mean they are here to stay for a good time yet; and hence that physical travel is also here to stay. Living 'life on the screen' is rarely a substitute for physical co-presence.

Finally, we considered how tourism seems to be increasingly about co-present meetings and less about just travelling to see the exotic. We showed the importance of meetings taking place within families, especially of migrants and diasporas, and that tourist-type travel is really as much about sociability as it is a search for exotic places. Thus, we have argued that it is necessary to de-exoticize tourism and travel theory. Tourist travel is not only an isolated 'exotic island' but often also a significant set of social and material relations. We have shown how these relations connect and reconnect 'disconnected' people in intermittent face-to-face meetings. Obligations and pleasures can go hand in hand. Thus whereas *sightseeing* used to be a fitting basis for tourism and travel theory, *networking* is now also an illuminating concept, although we do not intend to replace one with the other (see Chapter 7).

Various critiques were provided of existing ways of collecting data related to travel and meetings. Overall we set out various reasons why physical travel is necessarily intertwined with the very fabric of a rich, complex and occasionally mobile social life. This will be explored further in the next chapter on travel per se.

Chapter 4

Mobilities

Introduction

This chapter starts with a discussion of the five 'mobilities' that support social networks and generate travel demand in the contemporary world. While most research focuses upon one of these it is crucial to examine the interconnections *between* these different mobilities. Following that we briefly set out a framework for establishing just why people physically travel given the array of alternatives now available. We then note some evident inequalities of access to travel and hence of the capacity to meet up. We also discuss the scale of travel, and how the distribution of travel resources is highly unequal. We finally consider the hypotheses of substitution and complementarity between communications and physical travel, within the specific context of mobile workers, teleworkers and the coordination of everyday mobility and meetings.

Five Interdependent Mobilities

The five interdependent mobilities are (for more detail see Urry 2002, 2003):

- *Physical travel* of people for work, leisure, family life, pleasure, migration, and escape. Travel is embodied as people's need to be physically in the same space as various others, including workmates, business colleagues, friends, partner or family, or to encounter bodily some particular landscape or townscape, or to be physically present at a particular live event. Travel results in intermittent moments of physical proximity to particular peoples, places or events and that proximity is felt to be obligatory, appropriate, desirable or inevitable.
- *Physical movement* of objects to producers, consumers and retailers. This transports faraway objects and goods to where people live and/or work. It especially results from how the world is placed on display and then consumed within local supermarkets, restaurants, shopping malls and so on.
- *Imaginative travel* elsewhere through memories, texts, images, TV and films (see Larsen 2004). This travel will often substitute for physical transport, as analysed in de Botton's *The Art of Travel* (2002). There are 1 billion TV sets worldwide; TV enables people to attend live events without leaving the armchair or the local pub. Over the last two years there has been a decline in the number of football supporters that travel to see their team play away while

there has been a noticeable increase in supporters that attend away games at the local bar[1]. But imaginative travel also produces desires for travel and for tourist destinations. For instance, major films and soap operas often cause large tourist flows where few roamed before the location was made visible on the silver screen (Tooke and Baker 1996; Riley, Baker and Van Doren 1998; Tzanelli 2004; Couldry 2005; Crouch, Jackson and Thompson 2005). This enables tourism to invent many new destinations. According to media scholar Couldry, there has been an upsurge in 'media pilgrimage', which: 'is both a real journey across space, and an acting out in space of the constructed "distance" between "ordinary world" and "media world"' (2005, 72).

- *Virtual travel* often in real time on the internet, so transcending geographical and social distance. By 2003, two-thirds of the UK adult population were internet users. People are able to 'plug into' global networks of information through which they can 'do' things to at least certain objects (especially with increasing bandwidth), without their bodies having to travel physically. If people bank electronically they are able to access their money in many parts of the world; if people want to work on texts with others they can do so from any networked computer; if people want to buy a book they can order it at Amazon and save the trip to the local or the specialized bookstore a good drive away. Some commentators suggest that virtual travel may mean the end to traditional tourism: 'Why fly to a Las Vegas casino-hotel when one can play the slots and other games of chance on line? Why go to the racetrack when one can bet on the races over the Internet?' (Ritzer 2001, 147; see also Rojek 1997; Larsen 2004; Molz 2006).

- *Communicative travel* through person-to-person messages via letters, postcards, birthday and Christmas cards, telegrams, telephones, faxes, emails, instant messages and videoconferences. Social network members with internet access are but an *email away* and members with mobile phones stay connected even when they are on the move. Communicative travel also allows the digital transport of documents and photographs as attachments to email, thus substituting for the postal service. Emails are particular powerful in travelling the world: they travel long distances as fast as short ones; they travel equally fast and equally cheaply to multiple destinations ('lists') as to single ones. Email address books, lists and practices of sending, replying and not least forwarding emails mean that news, gossip, jokes, job information, conference calls and scandals can travel the world in a small-worldly way with incredible speed, and since emails travel digitally their movement is less marked through space (Hamill 2005; Kibby 2005; see Watters 2004, 114–45, for the swift travelling of a Nike scandal).[2] Moreover, there are now more mobile phones

---

1   http://www.footballeconomy.com/rep_oct_16.htm.
2   Kibby brings out the mobile nature of email:

The development of email has allowed for the rapid and effortless dissemination of information. Emails can [travel] as fast as required: it is not delayed by geographic distance or difference in time

than landlines and, in May 2003, according to National Statistics,[3] 75 per cent of adults in UK owned or used a mobile phone, and in 2001 the total number of mobile phones worldwide for the first time surpassed the number of TVs (Katz and Aakhus 2002a; Geser 2004). There are now 3.2 billion mobile phone users worldwide. The overall volume of international telephone calls increased at least tenfold between the early 1982 and 2001 (Vertovec 2004, 223). 'In December 2004, 2.4 billion text messages were sent in Britain as the traditional Christmas card was dumped in favour of a seasonal text message'.[4] Perhaps more than anything else, the last few years have seen a huge increase in a new kind of writing culture with the popularity of email and text messaging. The triumph of this new writing culture results from its fast and frictionless movement through social and geographical space; it seems designed for those on the move (Geser 2004).

The mobile phone shows how these different mobilities intersect. It seems that few people in the rich 'North and West' undertake physical travel without their mobile phone (probably manufactured in China or another low-cost production country) to fill those empty moments, at bus stops, to kill time on long journeys by chatting away and to organize meeting-places and times. So, as an object, the mobile phone itself travels, and it affords communicative mobility, as well as imaginative mobility and virtual mobility (through making and transporting photographs and video sequences).

In the rest of this chapter we discuss various dimensions of the physical travel of people, bringing out connections with the other mobilities adumbrated above.

Scale of Travel

In 2004 there were a record 760 million legal international passenger arrivals. This compares with 25 million in 1950, 700 million in 2002, with a predicted 1 billion by 2010 and more than 1.5 billion in 2020.[5] Travel and tourism is the largest industry in the world, accounting for 11.7 per cent of world GDP, 8 per cent of world exports and 8 per cent of employment. Side-by-side with global tourists and travellers are 31 million refugees and 100 million international migrants worldwide. Such exiles are

---

zones; it does not require coordination between sender and receiver; as an electronic document it is amenable to the full range of computer-based tools and applications and can be easily filed, modified, updated and edited; it is achieved by default and can be retrieved at any time; and it is ostensibly economical. These characteristics have made email one of the dominant methods of communication, not only within organizations such as business, government and education, but as a primary means of communicating among families and friends. (2005, 771)

3   http://www.statistics.gov.uk/StatBase/ssdataset.asp?vlnk=7202&Pos=4&Pos=4&Col Ranl=2&Ra.

4   http://www.text.it/mediacentre/default.asp?intPageID=132.

5   www.world-tourism.org/newsroom/Releases/2005/January/2004numbers.htm.

fleeing from famine, war, torture, persecution and genocide, as economic and social inequalities and consequential displacements of population have magnified in recent years and have forced travel upon many (Papastergiadis 1999, 10, 41, 54). Tourists, workers, terrorists, students, migrants, asylum seekers, scientists, scholars, family members, business people, soldiers and guest workers still travel under different circumstances, so we should differentiate between different forms of physical travel and understand how they are caught in various power geometries of everyday life (Massey 1994; Cresswell 2001; Hannam, Sheller and Urry 2006). As Massey says: 'Different social groups have distinct relationships to this anyway differentiated mobility: some people are more in charge of it than others; some initiate flows and movement, others don't; some are more on the receiving end of it than others; some are effectively imprisoned by it' (1994, 149).

Such patterns of physical travel seem to be affecting almost everywhere. The World Tourism Organization publishes tourism statistics for 220 countries,[6] with almost everywhere being either a significant sender or receiver of visitors, or both, although the flows are extremely uneven. Whereas disposable incomes in Western Europe and the United States have substantially increased within recent decades, airfares in real terms have declined (Frändberg and Vilhelmson 2003, 1755). The introduction of no-frills/low-cost airlines has made air travelling much cheaper and more widespread. Thus 'no-frills is the fastest-growing sector of the airline industry in Europe, which, analysts say, could triple in the next five years' (Collis cited in Davidson and Cope 2003, 43). Airfares in the UK fell by 30 per cent in 2002 (Tarry 2003, 82). While the costs of cars have stagnated during the last decades, the quality adjusted purchase costs also continued to decline (Axhausen 2005b, 3–4).

People in Britain are travelling five times further per year than in the 1950s. This figure is expected to double again by 2025. So far this principally results from car travel, which has set in train novel kinds of family life, community, leisure, the pleasures of movement and so on, principally involving new movement and not the replacement of other transport by the car (Adams 1999, 12; Vigar 2002; Urry 2004a; Featherstone, Thrift and Urry 2005). UK citizens currently each make around 1,000 trips a year, a figure that seems fairly constant (Doyle and Nathan 2001). Most trips are to destinations that could not be reached when bicycles and trains were the main forms of transport.[7] In the late 1890s the average commuting distance was 3.6 km and took 17.7 minutes. In the 1930s and 1940s, when public transport dominated, the average commuting distance increased to around 7–8 km and took around 34 minutes to complete. By the 1990s when around one in two commuting trips are made by car the average one-way journey to work had increased to 14.6 km and took 34.5 minutes. Thus between the 1930s and the 1990s, while commuting distances more than doubled, commuting times increased by less than five minutes (Pooley and Turnbull 2000a, 366; 2000b; see also Pooley, Turnbull and Adams 2005; but see

---

6   www.world-tourism.org.facts/metho.html.

7   In the UK today only 2% of journeys are by bike, compared with 20% in a bike-friendly country such as Denmark (*Independent* 6 February 2005).

Van Wee, Rietveld and Meurs, 2006, for an analysis of growing travel times in the Netherlands).

Thus people are travelling further and faster but neither more often nor spending much more time actually on the road. On average, each person travelled 6.833 miles per day in 2003 compared with 4.476 miles in 1972/1973 (DfT 2004, Table 1). The average time spent travelling each day has remained at around one hour per person for the past three decades, as has the average trip time of around 22 minutes (Schafer and Victor 2000, 271; DfT 2004; Lyons and Urry 2005).

The UK Innovation and Performance Unit indicates that most everyday journeys take place within a radius of eight or nine miles, so day-to-day physical travel is relatively local (Donovan, Pilch and Rubenstein 2002). However, 8–9-mile journeys or commuting 10–11 miles (the average commuting distance) are for most impossible by foot (by modern Western standards). They both require fit and keen cyclists, or a well-serviced public transport system. So car cultures transform what we mean by 'local' and indeed what are the short distances to travel.

This same report also shows that people mostly drive to see friends and family members – almost 40 miles a week. So much travel is 'social' travel. Similar German research indicates that leisure and holidays are the most significant trips with respect to miles travelled, and the meeting of friends and relatives is the most common reason for travelling (Schlich et al 2004, 225; and see Chapter 9 below). Thus many people will drive fairly long distances to see their non-local friends, a couple of times each month. So while most people on a day-to-day basis make short trips, they intermittently embark on longer leisure journeys to socialize with others at-a-distance. Of all long distance journeys in UK, 47 per cent are to visit family and friends (for a couple of days) (Dateline 2003, 17, 57; see also Schlich, Simma and Axhausen 2003), and almost half the UK population travels several hundred miles or more when they go abroad for their foreign holidays. This again illustrates how we cannot determine the geographical mobility of people and their networks without examining intermittent tourist-type long-distance travel.

Why Travel?

How can we explain these increases in the scale of physical travel? It is evident that people undertake long-distance travel for many reasons and under different circumstances: attending business meetings, conferences and job interviews; commuting to work; going abroad to study; migrating; escaping poverty, war and torture; visiting friends and family members; embarking on pilgrimages; going on holiday and so on. The developing and fulfilling of such activities and networks means that travel is necessary for social life, enabling complex connections to be made between workmates, leisure groups, crime networks, professional associations, voluntary associations, family or friends. There are various social obligations and burdens of apparently free mobility (Shove 2002). People's patterns of travel are choreographed by circumstances not completely of their own making.

We can summarize these obligations and motivations of travel within the following fivefold schema. First, travel occurs for legal, economic and familial obligations. These are either to specific persons (bride to groom) or to generic types of people (all who knew the late Mr Smith). These formal obligations include travel to go to work; to attend a family event such as a wedding, christening, or funeral, Christmas, Easter and so on; to meet a legal obligation by visiting a lawyer or court; to have to visit a school, hospital, university or public office; or to attend a job interview.

Second, there are less formally prescribed social obligations involving very strong normative expectations of presence and attention. This mutual presence enables each to read what the other seems to be really thinking, to observe their body language, to hear 'first hand' what they have to say, to sense directly their overall response, to undertake some emotional work. Such social obligations to friends or family are essential for developing those relations of trust that persist during often long periods of distance and even solitude. These social obligations are associated with obligations to spend moments of 'quality time' often within very specific locations often involving lengthy travel away from normal patterns of work and family life. There is often a quite distinct temporal feel to the moment, separate from and at odds with the normal processes of work, leisure and family life.

Third, there are object obligations. Such obligations include the necessity to be co-present to sign contracts or to work on or to see various objects, technologies or written texts. Such obligations to be co-present with objects often necessitates being within a specific kind of environment and this may necessitate particular kinds of design, security, comfort and ambience.

Fourth, there are obligations to place, to sense of place or a certain kind of place. Many places need to be seen for oneself, to be experienced directly: to meet at a particular house, say, of one's childhood or visit a particular restaurant or walk along a certain river valley or climb a particular hill or capture a good photograph or feel ones hands touching a rock-face and so on. It is only then that we know what a place is really like.

Fifth, there are event obligations – to experience a particular live event programmed to happen at a specific moment, including political rallies, concerts, plays, matches, celebrations, film premieres, festivals and so on. Each of these generates intense moments of co-presence. This is a kind of travel to place where timing is everything. These events cannot be missed and they set up enormous demands for mobility at very specific moments (but they can sometimes be substituted by watching TV).

Inequalities in Travel

The opportunities for travel are highly unequal. Being on the move has radically different implications for the businessman, the all-inclusive package tourist, the imported sex worker, the mobile professional, the asylum seeker and the backpacker. Access to (the right sort of) mobility has become a major stratifying factor, as Bauman has described:

Alongside the emerging planetary dimensions of business, finance, trade and information flow, a 'localising', space-fixing process is set in motion ... What appears as globalisation for some means localisation for others; signalling a new freedom for some, upon many others it descends as an uninvited and crucial fate. Mobility climbs to the rank of the uppermost among the coveted values – and the freedom to move, perpetually a scarce and unequally distributed commodity, fast becomes the main stratifying factor of our late-modern or postmodern times. (1998, 2)

In the UK the richest quintile travels 3.5 times further than the poorest quintile. One-half of UK adults took a flight during 2001, with one-half travelling once, one-quarter travelling twice and one-quarter travelling three or more times a year (Lethbridge 2002). If international mobility was equally distributed in Sweden each person would go abroad once a year (Frändberg and Vilhelmson 2003, 1762). In fact, in Sweden a small group of hypermobile people, comprising a mere 3 per cent of the population, makes up almost 25 per cent of international journeys, partly because they undertake 60 per cent of international business trips. This group make more than five international journeys per year. Since 'hypermobility' is closely related to business travel, males, high-income earners and city dwellers dominate this category. Almost half the population in Sweden do not fly at all each year, while 28 per cent embark upon one non-domestic journey. So, in terms of international mobility, 75 per cent of Swedes are 'nonmobile' or only 'slightly mobile' (Frändberg and Vilhelmson 2003, 1762–3).

Moreover around 45 per cent of the UK population lives and works within five miles of where they were born (Doyle and Nathan 2001) (this does not necessarily mean that they have always lived there: see Chapter 6). These are mainly people with lower educational credentials, whereas graduates are more likely to live elsewhere. Thus people with higher-level qualifications, especially university degrees, are more geographically mobile:

Only 12% of graduates live in the same local authority as they were born – compared with 44% of the general population. There may be two reasons for this. First the act of going to university may break the link with the person's parental region. Second, the labour market for graduates is a national one – with jobs advertised in the national press and specialist publications. For those with lower skill levels jobs tend to be advertised locally, and people tend to find out about jobs through informal networks of friends and family. (Donovan, Pilch and Rubenstein 2002, 9)

Other research indicates that 'stranded mobility' can occur for those living in poverty (Grieco and Raje 2004). Many low-income housing areas have experienced a cut back in transport services. At the same time, bus fares have increased considerably and made buses relatively more expensive than travelling by car. This is so despite the fact that 'those without cars usually need more time, greater effort and pay a higher marginal cost to reach the same destination as people with cars' (DETR report, cited in Kenyon, Lyons and Rafferty 2002, 220). This has major consequences for these people and lone-mother households in particular, of which the majority live in poverty and without a car (Allan and Crow 2001, 136). Lack of reliable, frequent and well-connected transport reduces access and connectivity to social networks and necessary social activities. For instance, 'there is evidence that choice of job, or even the possibility of taking a job at all ... can be constrained by mobility difficulties, in particular for part-time and shift work, low skilled and low paid jobs' (Kenyon, Lyons and Rafferty 2002, 10). There is clear evidence of 'mobility divides' in Western societies (Cass, Shove and Urry 2003, 2005; Schönfelder and Axhausen 2003). These inequalities can also be reinforced by the 'digital divide', with only 7 per cent of households in the lowest income decile having access to the internet, compared with 71 per cent in the highest decile. People and households facing physical mobility-related exclusion are also likely to suffer from virtual mobility-related exclusion (Kenyon, Lyons and Raferty 2002, 221). However, the ownership of mobile phones is an exception here, as virtually every (at least youngish) person in the UK possesses at least one (and see Katz and Aakhus 2002a).

Travelling and Communicating

In this section we discuss whether communication technologies substitute for physical travel, being cheaper and faster. Are communication technologies a tool to reduce traffic congestion, air pollution, and many problems related to the burning of fossil fuel? The literature here is considerable (and some was discussed in the previous chapter in the context of meetings: see Cairncross 1997; Graham 1998; Mokhtarian 1990, 2003; Golob and Regan 2001; Vilhelmson and Thulin 2001; Cairns et al 2004; Gillespie and Richardson 2004; Plaut 2004).

There are contrasting hypotheses: substitution or complementarity. Plaut argues that transport researchers and professionals generally predict major substitution of transportation by communication via the internet or the phone (2004, 163). Transport researchers argue that:

> As we become busier, we will increasingly rely on IT to avoid unnecessary travel ... Also, as we spend new time engaged in telecommunications, there will simply be less time available for other activities, including travel. Small effects by a very large number of persons will aggregate up to large effects on a system wide basis. (Golob and Regan 2001, 114)

According to the substitution thesis, telecommunicating, teleconferencing, telemeeting, tele-education (distance learning), telebanking, teleshopping and other telesubstitutions will replace corporeal travel (Mokhtarian 2003, 45). So this thesis is closely related to the idea that 'geography is dead' – distance no longer much matters.

The complementarity hypothesis involves the idea of enhancement and increased efficiency. Rather than replacing physical transport of people and objects, communication technologies make the planning and coordination of travel more efficient and smoother. So, rather than substituting for physical travel, it will enhance its volume. To cite Plaut:

News of the demise of location and transportation appears be premature. Those who believe that advanced telecommunications and information technologies have made geography and distance irrelevant appear to be mistaken. If anything, more communications appear to be producing more an expanded use of the transportation system, and vice versa. (2004, 165)

Communication objects and technologies potentially make journeys more effective in another sense too; they afford the transformation of planes, trains and even cars into workplaces, and wasteful travel time into productive work time (Brown 2002; Brown and O'Hara 2003; Laurier and Philo 2003, Letherby and Reynolds 2003; Laurier 2004a, 2004b; Lyons and Urry 2005). As Laurier points out:

On my laptop I can carry my diary, my address book, several hundred downloaded articles, all my previous publications, the majority of my correspondence, grant application forms, an offline version of my website, a thousand or more photos, some of my favourite records, a few episodes of a TV show ... In other words in my shoulder bag I can carry a large proportion of my office and study which in paper form and as vinyl LPs and video-cassettes would have filled a small van. How odd, really, to imagine that if academics could carry their libraries with them in a shoulder bag that they would travel less? (2004a, 3)

So here mobile information and communication technologies are seen as enabling people to be more mobile in relation to work and leisure, to become 'digital nomads'. Trains, buses, cars, streets and waiting lounges are now places of communication and where travel time can be made productive (Lyons and Urry 2005). The mobile phone seems to be the most useful device for those working on the move, providing important communications with co-workers and clients (Laurier 2004b). Over a fifth of rail passengers thought that having such devices with them made the time on the train a lot better (though nearly half of all passengers, 46 per cent, considered that electronic devices had not made the travel time any better). Those travelling first class were more likely to consider that such communication devices made their time use more effective (Lyons, Jain and Holley 2005).

Other research suggests that new social routines are engendering spaces that are 'in between' home, work and social life, forming 'interspaces' (Hulme and Truch 2004). These are places of intermittent movement where groups come together, involving the use of phones, mobiles, laptops, SMS messaging, wireless communications and so on, often to make arrangements on the move. Some 'meetings' consist of 'underground' social gatherings or 'smart mobs' located in between the formal locations of work or home (Rheinholdt 2002).

Various workplace studies examine the spatial practices and communication technologies that mobile workers – 'hot-deskers' – carry out and employ to make non-workplaces such as cars, trains and waiting rooms workable, rather like offices (Heath, Knoblauch and Luff 2000; Brown and O'Hara 2003; Laurier and Philo 2003; Laurier 2004a, 2004b). Hot-deskers do not have a permanent office and it is expected of them that they work not only at home and in clients' offices but also on the move. Such mobile workers manage their working-in-travelling in such way that they plan their activities and work tasks according to the varied physical environments where they will work: 'So all the e-mailing might be done when in the office, or all the reading done when on the train. In this respect we can see how place is an important determinant in the ordering of work activities for the mobile worker' (Brown and O'Hara 2003, 1571).

The flexible car, the network-connected laptop computer, the mobile telephone are crucial in making places workable (Laurier 2004b). The first of these enables flexible transportation, the second one affords access to documents, files, and emails, while the third allows connectivity to other colleagues and clients (Brown and O'Hara 2003, 1576). The car is transformed into an office through its combination with the mobile phone and mobile computing, enabling the 'car-assemblage' to become a more effective mobile office. Work materials are synchronized and connected up to other company members while one is on the road. The mobile phone and car-based telematics function as 'actants', taking messages as voicemail, screening calls, and providing information about traffic delays and alternative routes (especially with the increasing merging of various car-based mobile communications). The mobile is regularly used to rearrange the day as traffic can impede the planned series of meetings and encounters (see Ling and Yttri 2002). Teamworking is achieved by the skilful use of mobile telephony so as to maintain connections and synchronize timetables both with those back at the office (including making meeting arrangements, dictating letters and so on), as well as with those others who are elsewhere on the road and with whom meetings can be arranged. Thus an essential practical temporal concern for mobile workers is to achieve synchronicity in events across time and space. Meetings might occur at motorway service stations, roadside cafés, pubs, restaurants and so on.

Interestingly, paper documents (printed agendas, printed emails, faxes, printed illustrations and so on) are normally crucial for mobile working and meetings (as we also found in finalizing this book at-a-distance!). Mobile workers often read and make comments on hard copies rather than on the screen. Whereas laptops can be cumbersome and rigid in meeting situations, paper documents afford 'a high level of micro-mobility ... around the meeting space that made it a useful conversational resource'. They allow scribbling in margins, can be passed around a room, photocopied and so on (Brown and O'Hara 2003, 1576). Likewise, paper documents are frequently used for ad hoc reading activities between meetings and travelling. The paperless office is thus a 'myth' in relationship to the mobile office.

The substitution and complementarity theses have been discussed intensively in relation to teleworking. An early study by Gillespie and Richardson concluded that some teleworking might enhance rather than substitute work-related travel, even though such workers do not commute on a daily basis to a permanent office:

> Despite the sophisticated supporting electronic networks, face-to-face meetings are still required, both with clients and with other team members, but now instead of popping next door to meet work colleagues, or travelling a few miles to meet clients, workers have to

travel up and down the motorway on a regular basis. We would therefore anticipate that team teleworking, in expanding the geographical spread of participants in the virtual work activity space, is likely to lead to new demands for travel and to substantial increases in the distances over which business travel takes place. (Gillespie and Richardson 2004, 215)

A recent report for the Department for Transport (Cairns et al 2004) shows how teleworking can also reduce work-related transport, not least with regard to commuting to and from the workplace. Because these employees (for example, those working for BT) were little engaged in face-to-face meetings, the kilometres avoided by not commuting into the office complex were saved by spending more time on the road to meet up with other home-working or teleworking colleagues and clients, as predicted by Gillespie and Richardson. It seems that the transport-reducing effects of teleworking is predominately related to the types of service and knowledge jobs that, for shorter or longer periods, can be performed with a broadband connection, access to a computer network at work, telephone calls and perhaps teleconferencing, but with little need for co-present meetings and thick communications. So managers and executives are still likely to work in a sea of face-to-face interactions within office complexes. It is lower-rung workers with routinized IT tasks that are likely to be forced to work more or less permanently from their home, as companies free up expensive office space. Such workers who already have experienced a de-personalization of their communication practices with clients and customers (from face-to-face to face-to-interface) now work in 'de-personalized' environments without much collegial interaction and support. Home-working and even mobile teleworking can contribute further to what has been called the 'uneven access to ordinary talk' (Boden and Molotch 1994, 275).

In the next section we explore more broadly how communication technologies are intricately tied up with coordinating networks and everyday mobility.

Coordinating Networks and Travel

Although travel has both a spatial and a temporal dimension, transport and mobility research pays most attention to the spatial aspects and therefore to trains, ships, cars and planes. But travel is not merely about getting there but also about coordinating travel and arriving at the right time, at that specific moment when the meeting, match, wedding, funeral or dinner commence. Travel and meetings require systems of coordination and mobile communications that enable dispersed network members to bring together agendas, destinations and arrival before and during travel (Townsend 2004; Fortunati 2005; Jarvis 2005). Travel is not so much a question of movement but rather of spacing and timing (Shove 2002). Coordinating travel or meetings are thus both a spatial and temporal practice, and, thus, space and time cannot be analysed separately when investigating mobility or social life more generally (Bauman 2000b; May and Thrift 2001). More generally, in societies where social networks are stretched out and distant connections are common, it is difficult to meet up spontaneously and networks depend much upon systems of coordination, as Simmel (1997) famously analysed.

Simmel writes that the metropolitan type of personality consists of 'the *intensification of nervous stimulation* which results from the swift and uninterrupted change of outer and inner stimuli' (1997, 175). The modern city involves the 'unexpectedness of onrushing impressions ... With each crossing of the street, with the tempo and multiplicity of economic, occupational and social life', he says that the city sets up a 'deep contrast with small town and rural life with reference to the sensory foundations of psychic life' (Simmel 1997, 175). The onrushing stimulations create a new psychic and sensory configuration, the blasé attitude, the inability to react to new sensations with appropriate energy. The movement of the city generates reserve and indifference.

Moreover, because of the effect of money with 'all its colourlessness and indifference' (Simmel 1997, 178), but also because of its twin, the modern city, a new precision comes to be necessary in such a life. Agreements and arrangements need to demonstrate unambiguousness in timing and location. Life in the mobile onrushing city presupposes punctuality and this is reflected, according to Simmel, by the 'universal diffusion of pocket watches' (1997, 177). The watch was a century ago as symbolic of the 'modern' as the ubiquitous mobile phone is today. Simmel argues that the 'relationships and affairs of the typical metropolitan usually are so varied and complex that without the strictest punctuality in promises and services the whole structure would break down into an inextricable chaos' (1997, 177). This necessity for punctuality: 'is brought about by the aggregation of so many people with such differentiated interests who must integrate their relations and activities into a highly complex organism' (Simmel 1997, 177). In particular Simmel asserts that:

> If all clocks and watches in Berlin would suddenly go wrong in different ways, even if only by one hour, all economic life and communication of the city would be disrupted for a long time. Thus, the technique of metropolitan life is unimaginable without the most punctual integration of all activities and mutual relations into a stable and impersonal time schedule. (1997, 177)

Thus the forming of complex systems of relationships mean that meetings and activities have to be punctual, timetabled, rational, a system or 'structure of the highest impersonality' often involving much distance-keeping politeness (Simmel 1997, 178; Toiskallio 2002, 171). This 'system-ness' of mobility is crucial and results in the individual becoming 'a mere cog in an enormous organization of things and powers'; as a result 'life is made infinitely easy for the personality in that stimulations, interests, uses of time and consciousness are offered to it from all sides' (Simmel 1997, 184). Simmel tellingly notes how as a consequence: '[T]hey carry the person as if in a stream, and one needs hardly to swim for oneself' (1997, 184).

But simultaneously city life produces people with a 'highly personal subjectivity', a tendency to be 'different', of standing out in a striking manner and thereby seeking attention (Simmel 1997, 178). Urban life produces what we now call a pronounced 'culture of narcissism' (Lasch 1980). Simmel argues that people gain self-esteem through being aware of how they are specifically perceived by others. But because of the scale of mobility in the metropolis there is a 'brevity and scarcity of inter-human contacts' (Simmel 1997, 183). Compared with the small-scale community, the modern city gives room to the individual and to the peculiarities of their inner and outer development. It is the spatial form of modern urban life that permits the unique development of individuals who interact socially with an exceptionally wide range of contacts forming a distinct set of networks. People seek to distinguish themselves; to be different through adornment and fashion and encountering each other in brief moments of proximity.

So metropolitan life, its rush and fragmentation, generates both powerful objective systems partly concerned with maintaining rules of distance and formality, *and* very varied personal subjectivities. According to Simmel, 'one nowhere feels as lonely and lost as in the metropolitan crowd' and when travelling by public transport:

> The feeling of isolation is rarely as decisive and intense when one actually finds oneself physically alone, as when one is a stranger, without relations, among many physically close persons, at a 'party' on a train or in the traffic of a large city. (Simmel cited in Wolff 1950, 119)

While the early modern metropolis, on the one hand, produced people with a 'highly personal subjectivity', it produced objective systems of punctuality and pocket watches that isolated people in 'distance-keeping politeness', on the other. Simmel's work thus highlights how 'personalization' makes people depend upon complex systems and inflexible time.

The pocket watch was just one of many early modern 'systems'. The invention of organized leisure travel and tourism in the mid-nineteenth century relied upon the standardized time of Greenwich Mean Time, timetables and pocket watches (Lash and Urry 1994; see also Green 2002; Klein 2004). Everyday mobility in early twentieth-century cities such as Berlin was above all by public transport, which means that punctuality had to be assured. So pocket watches *and* public transport were early modern twins.

Another technology of that period was the landline telephone that allowed communications with absent others. But the *landline* phone confined talk at-a-distance to homes and offices. So people had to stay put when undertaking 'communicative travel'. In the era of pocket watches, public transport and landlines, meetings had to be organized in painstaking detail and people had to know their route and to arrive on time in the right place. The objective, unbending time of pocket watches determined whether people arrived successfully. They were equally inflexible and part of the same pre-mobile phone coordination system that we can characterize as *clock time punctuality*.

In Chapter 3 we discussed how mobile phones and networked individualism enable people to be in communicative propinquity with their social networks when they are absent and on the move. Research has yet to investigate fully how mobile phone cultures are changing how people arrange and attend meetings. In the era of landline phones, rigid planning was essential as people were unconnectable when away from home. The mobile phone eliminates this need for inflexible pre-coordination as people can arrange and rearrange their meetings on the move. Mobile 'phone spaces' afford informal, fluid and instantaneous ways of meeting up where venue, time, group and agenda can change with the next text message:

> The old schedule of minutes, hours, days, and weeks becomes shattered into a constant stream of negotiations, reconfigurations, and rescheduling. One can be interrupted or interrupt friends and colleagues at any time. Individuals live in this phonespace they can never let it go, because it is their primary link to the temporally, spatially fragmented network of friends and colleagues they have constructed for themselves. (Townsend 2004, 10)

Conclusion

In this chapter we set out the five main forms of mobility and then specifically examined the physical movement of people, showing some connections with these other mobilities. We then considered what it is that provokes such travel. We argued that there are five bases to travel, linking the debate back to the discussion in the previous chapter that deals with the importance of co-present meetings. We argued that we can conceptually distinguish between obligations to people, to places, to objects and to events, that some travel consists of combinations of these forms of obligation, and that each form results in a powerful need to be bodily present with those people, in that place, with that object, at that event.

We then noted some evident inequalities of access to travel and hence of the capacity to meet up. We considered the substitution and complementarity theses with regard to communications and physical travel, and showed that so far there are good reasons to believe that physical travel will continue its growing significance not only in relationship to business and professional travel, but also in relationship to teleworking, family life and emerging forms of friendship. We might see this as a process of co-evolution, between new forms of social networking on the one hand, and extensive forms of physical travel now often enhanced by new communications, on the other. In particular, communication technologies seem very important in the temporal coordination of meetings and travel, which we exemplified indirectly through the classical sociological work of Simmel. These sets of processes reinforce and extend each other in ways that are difficult to reverse.

This also means that crucial to the character of modern societies is something that we term *network capital* (see also Kaufmann 2003; Kaufmann, Manfred and Joye 2004). Those social groups that are high in network capital enjoy significant advantages within the systems of social inequality operating in the contemporary world. As mobilities are more central to social life, so access to network capital is of greater significance in the structuring of social inequality (as Bauman 2000a, brings out).

Network capital comprises six elements that together produce a distinct stratification order that sits alongside social class, social status and party (M. Weber 1948, Chapter 7):

- *Movement competences*: to walk distances within different environments, to board different means of mobility, to carry or move baggage, to read timetabled information, to access computerized information, to arrange and rearrange connections and meetings, the ability to use mobile phones, text messaging, email, the internet, skype, etc.
- *Location-free information and contact points*: sites where information and communications can arrive, be stored and retrieved (includes real/electronic diaries, address books, secretary, office, answering service, email, websites, mobile phones).
- *Communication devices*: to make and remake arrangements especially on the move and in conjunction with others also on the move. Email accounts and mobile phones are of particular significance here (and see Chapter 8).
- *Appropriate, safe and secure meeting-places:* both en route and at the destination(s), including office, club space, hotel, public spaces, street corner, café, interspaces.
- *Physical and financial access* to an email account, the internet, free phone calls at work, car, roadspace, fuel, lifts, aircraft, trains, ships, taxis, buses, trams, minibuses and so on.
- *Time/money/resources to manage and coordinate the others:* especially when there is system failure, as will intermittently happen.
- *Friends and family members at-a-distance* that offer their hospitality so that places can be visited cheaply and distant social networks can be maintained through intermittent visits (see Chapter 7).

In the empirical research reported below we investigate various social groups, some of which enjoy high levels of network capital – but not especially high levels of economic capital. We will see how their lives, partially on the move, come to be organized from day to day, week to week, year to year, how they can substitute for limited economic capital high levels of network capital (see Bourdieu 1984, generally on different forms of capital and their substitutability), and how this network capital is intricately intertwined with multiple technologies of movement, communications and meetings.

Chapter 5

Research Design

Introduction

This research empirically explores to what degree youngish people's social networks in the North-West of England[1] are stretched out geographically and what the consequences are of this spread for social life and likely future travel patterns. We discuss how we employ both existing methods and develop new ones in order to measure and represent the spatial nature of networks and networking practices.

We begin with describing this sample in terms of sex, occupation, education, income, age and marital status. Then the recruitment and the places of interviews are discussed. We justify the design of the interview guide and questionnaires and how they worked out in practice. This is followed by a discussion of how the raw data were analysed and represented as quotations, tables, figures and maps. In the conclusion we suggest how the research design could be improved upon within future research.

Interviewees

The focus here is upon three expanding occupations or industries that differ with regard to education, salary/status and expected mobility patterns. This research explores, to use Conradson and Latham's term, 'middling' forms of mobile life (2005b, 229). Rather than searching for mobile respondents per se, the following chapters examine to what degree distributed networks and mobile lives are characteristic of many people other than transnational elites and underprivileged migrants. We focus upon architects, employees in fitness centres (managers, sales staff, qualified instructors and receptionists) and security staff (university porters and nightclub doormen). Rather than undertaking our research in supposedly cosmopolitan London, we interview people in the North-West of England, respectively Manchester, Liverpool and Lancaster.

These particular occupations have rapidly expanded and are likely to continue to expand in the future. Thus the patterns found here indicate something about future trends. They are systematically selected for the light they cast on future social networks and travel patterns. Thus architectural jobs and practices have proliferated

---

1   North-West England is an English region. It covers 14,165 km^2 and has a population of 6,729,800. The main cities are Liverpool and Manchester (en.wikipedia.org/wiki/North_West_of_England).

and especially so in Manchester and Liverpool following the designation of the latter as European Capital of Culture for 2008. The fitness industry is booming and it has become common for people to be a member of a fitness club. This turn to the 'aesthetics of health and bodies' is likely to continue further as people, to paraphrase Putnam (2000), do fitness alone rather than join teams. The security industry is expanding because of (perceived) increases in 24-hour society requirements, terrorism, interpersonal violence, urban fears, the increased gating of housing estates, and the general privatizing of security.

Based upon the preceding chapters, our hypotheses are that:

- The architectural profession is highly mobile since architects move to study and work; they are rich in networking capital (car, email account, access to the internet and so on) and they will undertake long journeys for social networking;
- Managers and qualified instructors will demonstrate similar characteristics: they are mobile, moving residence to study and work, being rich in network capital and hence will undertake long journeys to meet up;
- Receptionists in the fitness industry and security staff are more likely to live relatively rooted lives with less residential, work-related and leisure mobility. They will exhibit relatively tight-knit and immobile networks with less network capital[2].

Recruitment of Interviewees

We interviewed 24 people. The invitation we distributed stated the purpose of the interview and of the overall research. We deliberately mentioned that it was not a requirement to have moved around a lot or to travel much to participate, but only to have a willingness to report upon one's social networks, of friends, family members and workmates for approximately two hours (see Larsen, Urry and Axhausen 2006).

Table 1 below illustrates the main characteristics of this sample. Nine architects work predominantly in Liverpool. Since the architectural profession is heavily male, we only managed to interview two women. Most of the architects are in their late twenties or early thirties and their average annual income is £28,000 (this excludes No. 9, an architectural student doing compulsory work placement). While seven out of nine have partners (six are married), none have children – this despite all being heterosexual. They are all white, two being born and bred outside the UK in Ireland (No. 5) and Russia (Russian citizen) (No. 2). These architects form a relative homogeneous group.

---

2   It should be noted that we do not trace networks as such, since we do not go on to interview the many 'links' that the interviewees identify. This would require very many further interviews.

There are nine interviewees working in the fitness industry in Manchester.[3] Three of these are women. This group is less homogeneous: the ages vary from early twenties to late thirties; four work in sales; two are receptionists; and three work as fitness instructors;[4] three have managerial positions and the managers and the sales staff are earning substantially more than the receptionists (both receptionists regard their jobs as a stop-gap). Title and salary are not related to university degree here as two of the sales advisers and one of the receptionists have university degrees, while this is not the case with any of the managers. However, they also have common characteristics. All are white, except one woman with Indian origins (No. 13); all are British citizens; and none have children.

The final group consists of six people working in the security industry in Lancaster: three porters and three nightclub doormen. There is an unequal distribution of the sexes; their ages range from 21 to 38. This group is typified by low salaries (just more than £10,000 annually on average) and the lack of university degrees. All are white with the exception of the female porter who is of Asian origin (No. 19). This woman and the doorman/gardener have children.

The average age of the whole sample is 28.5 years, while the mean salary is just above £20,000. There are six women and 18 men. There is a significant dominance of (heterosexual) couples with only four singles. We now continue by discussing the design of the interview guide and questionnaires.

Interview Guide and Questionnaires[5]

This research combines qualitative and quantitative methods to measure and visualize networks and networking practices on the one hand, and to examine people's multilayered accounts of why and how they network and what their networking means to them, on the other. All interviewees filled in two questionnaires and undertook a lengthy qualitative interview. We designed a detailed interview guide to make the interviews systematic and comparable. Each interview was designed to last for around two hours (for a detailed discussion, see Larsen, Urry and Axhausen 2006).

---

3   That the architects predominately work in Liverpool, while all the fitness centre employees are in Manchester is purely coincidental.

4   Interviewee No. 18 is now only working part time as a self-employed fitness instructor. She used to work full time on a cruise ship in the Caribbean but her main job today is as an air steward.

5   Our interview guide and questionnaires are included in the appendix to Larsen, Urry and Axhausen 2006.

Table 1   Summary description of the interviewees and the location of the interview

No	Profession	Sex	Age	Income	University degree	Relationship	Working in	Children	Interview conducted at
1	Architect	F	Early 30s	N/A	Yes	Married	Liverpool	No	Work
2	Architect	F	Early 30s	N/A	Yes	Partner	Liverpool	No	Bar
3	Architect	M	Early 30s	25,000	Yes	Married	Liverpool	No	Work
4	Architect	M	Early 30s	32,000	Yes	Single	Liverpool	No	Bar
5	Architect	M	Late 20s	N/A	Yes	Married	Liverpool	No	Work
6	Architect	M	Late 20s	27,000	Yes	Married	Manchester	No	Home
7	Architect	M	Late 20s	N/A	Yes	Married	Liverpool	No	Work
8	Architect	M	Mid 20s	24,000	Yes	Married	Liverpool	No	Work
9	Architect (student)	M	Early 20s	13,400	Yes	Single	Liverpool	No	Home
10	Sales adviser, fitness centre	M	Late 20s	20,000	Yes	Partner	Manchester	No	Work
11	Sales adviser, fitness centre	M	Late 20s	19,000	Yes	Partner	Manchester	No	Work
12	Receptionist, fitness centre	F	Early 20s	15,000	Yes	Partner	Manchester	No	Work
13	Receptionist, fitness centre	F	Mid 20s	13,000	No	Partner	Manchester	No	Work
14	Sales manager, fitness centre	M	Mid 20s	30,000	No	Partner	Manchester	No	Work
15	Fitness instructor manager	M	Mid 30s	19,000	No	Single	Manchester	No	Work
16	Fitness instructor manager	M	Mid 30s	22,000	No	Partner	Manchester	No	Work
17	Sales ass. in fitness centre	M	Mid 20s	16,000	No	Partner	Manchester	No	Work
18	Personal trainer/cabin crew	F	Mid 30s	18,000	No	Partner	Manchester	No	Cafe

Table 1   Continued

No	Profession	Sex	Age	Income	University degree	Relationship	Working in	Children	Interview conducted at
19	Porter	F	Late 30s	14,000	No	Married	Lancaster	Yes	Bar
20	Porter	M	Mid 30s	9,500	No	Partner	Lancaster	No	Work
21	Porter	M	Mid 20s	12,500	No	Married	Lancaster	No	Work
22	Doorman/student	M	Early 20s	11,000	Student	Single	Lancaster	No	Bar
23	Doorman/student	M	Early 20s	15,000	Student	Partner	Lancaster	No	Bar
24	Doorman/gardener	M	Mid 30s	N/A	No	Married	Lancaster	Yes	Researcher

Pre-interview Questionnaire

Before the formal interview, the interviewees filled in a 10–20 minute questionnaire that established their residential mobility in time and space – where (city and area) and with whom they lived during their school days and over the last 5–15 years (depending upon their age). It further establishes their access to networking tools (which is a significant aspect of what we have called network capital), the number of business and personal journeys they made in 2004 in the UK and abroad and the location of their non-local friends.

Interview Guide

The interview guide elicits respondents' communication practices, travel and face-to-face visits for work, friendship and family life. The interview guide highlights the *relational* webs of individual biographies. Our network analysis deals with single people (where each is an 'ego' in a wider network) so there is a danger of overemphasizing individualized accounts. To avoid this, the interviews examine the relational commitments and relationships that immobilize and mobilize people under specific circumstances. It covers how, and how often, emails, text messages and phone calls connect people in intimate phone-to-phone conversation, text-to-text gossip, email-to-email-to-email coordination and circulation and so on. We asked people to describe their emails and text messages, how far they travel and to how many places. Respondents are asked to describe how emails, text messages and phone calls function as networking tools, how they use them to gossip, flirt, tease, argue, exchange information and jokes, organize travel and face-to-face meetings and to 'get lost in conversation'.

Then the interview guide turns to geographies of travel. The interviewees are asked to describe the last long journeys they made within the UK and abroad. We ask not only where the respondents travel but also with whom they travel, who they visit and what social obligations they fulfil with this journey.

The interview guide also addresses geographies of old and new friends. Interviewees are asked where their friends live, how they first met and keep in contact as well as how often they meet and where, and how much travel this entails; whether the majority of their friends are close by or elsewhere; how important it is for them to be close to their friends and whether they think long-distance friendship works; what friendship obligations generate travel. We discussed to what degree distance and (travel and communication) costs constrain interaction and also how people have learned to live with a 'friction of distance' and networking at-a-distance.

Then we ask the same questions in relationship to family life. Interviewees are asked where their parents, sisters, brothers and grandparents reside; why they live close or far away from them; whether this was desirable or problematical, beneficial or inconvenient; whether they are likely to move closer or further away from their family in the future. Then we talk about how often the family meets up, at what occasions, and how much travel such visits involve, whether distance and cost of transport affect their rate of recurrent travel.

Post-interview Questionnaire

At the end of the interview, the interviewees are asked to complete another questionnaire, which again takes 10–20 minutes. Here interviewees are asked to identify the 'most important people' in their social networks (up to 10) and specify their residential location; when and how they meet; and how often they stay in contact by mail, phone, text message and face-to-face meetings. This identifies the geographical distribution of respondents' 'strong ties' (Granovetter, 1983).

Analysing and Visualizing the Data

The material generated by the interviews and questionnaires was turned into transcripts, a database, quotations, figures, tables and maps. The qualitative examination of the interviews is concerned with how networks are subjectively viewed, experienced and practised by interviewees, and how such individual accounts can be generalized so as to develop new theoretical insights. While this analysis is not concerned with quantitative questions we nonetheless try to identify what views are common, and when a quote is discussed, or used to exemplify a point in the following chapters, we roughly indicate how typical it is; we also quantify parts of the interviews. All quantifiable data in the interviews were coded and analysed in a statistical database specifically designed for this project[6] – alongside the information in the questionnaires – so we have been able to generate figures and tables out of otherwise qualitative interviews. This mix of qualitative and quantitative analysis is particular salient in Chapter 6, while Chapters 7 and 8 are predominantly qualitative.

In Chapter 6 we experiment with mapping techniques to illustrate the spatial reach of each respondent's social networks (this approach was suggested by Schönfelder and Axhausen 2003). We determine how geographically dispersed the respondents' networks are by measuring how far away they live from their 'non-local friends', 'close family members' and their 'most important people'.[7] All reported locations were located by longitude and latitude, that is, geocoded. Using these coordinates we calculated the 'great circle distance' between them based upon the spherical shape of the Earth (Hubert and Potier 2003). As we had only place names available, such as Liverpool or London, we cannot calculate the distance between the homes of people within the same city. These were set to zero.

In terms of mapping, the geocoded data was then incorporated into a geographic information system (GIS), which is basically a geographically aware database. Since

---

6   The data was captured with and stored with MS Access 2000. The tabulations were created with SPSS 13.

7   We only map current network geographies but this method could examine changing network geographies over time, if the data were available.

most networks are made up of both close by and faraway connections the maps constructed visualize ties on local, national and global scales. While the printed size of the maps is the same, the depicted areas in the local ties and global ties maps will be different from respondent to respondent, as we adjust the scale to fit the specific geographies of their ties (contrast Map 1 and Map 3).

As the legend explains, the maps contain information about the respondents' current place of residence, their most important people, other friends and family and former places of residence. The home of the respondent and the place of her/his connections are linked by coloured lines, and these also indicate the distances between them. We use black lines to connect the respondent to her/his most important people and blue lines to other friends and family. We trace the respondents' residential mobility over time and space with numbers and green lines. These lines are particularly helpful in visualizing distances, identifying 'hubs' and linking residential mobility with network geographies of friends and family members.

On each map there are five or six small boxes with details about some of the respondents' ties: their relationship (family member, friend, etc.); how long they have known each other; how often the phone, email, text and meet up; and the cost (money and time)[8] of meeting up in terms of travel.

Conclusion

In this chapter we have described the design of this research project, the results of which are reported in the next chapters. We suggest in future research that network technologies (websites, email accounts, laptops, mobile/camera-phones, digital cameras, voiceover-IP telephony, such as www.skype.com, diaries, PDA, iPod, MP3-player, etc.) and documents (emails and text messages containing tickets, invitations, travel information, photographs and post-meeting gossip) should play a more integrated role within such interviews. If such technologies and documents were at hand during the interview it would be easier to remember the journeys (destination, price, company, etc.) and meetings (with whom, how it was coordinated and through what means, etc.). This would have the positive side-effect that the researcher becomes less dependent upon oral accounts and can include text messages, emails and email attachments (e.g. tickets, photographs) in the final account as well as in ethnographic observations of how the respondents use communication technologies.

---

8 It is difficult to determine travel costs especially because there are large discounts when tickets are bought in advance. Since our interviewees normally buy their train tickets two weeks in advance to obtain maximum discount, we report fares for such tickets. Similarly, the reported flight tickets are booked three months in advance. Since our respondents fly budget airlines when possible, we began our search at Ryanair and Easyjet. If unsuccessful, we turned to the popular travel portal Expedia (www.expedia.co.uk) and searched for the cheapest deal booked three months in advanced. In relation to car journeys, we used AA Route Map to indicate time and actual travel distance (rather than great circle distance).

This will be particularly helpful in enhancing understanding of how communication technologies coordinate and occasionally substitute for travel.

Retrospectively, it is also clear that our interview guide at times focuses too much upon individuals. In relation to family life we neglect families-in-law, and how respondents' income partly depends upon what their partners earn or what gifts they derive from other family members.

Chapter 6

Geographies of Networks and Mobilities

Introduction

We argued that mobilities of talk, writing and meetings sustain social networks, networks that potentially spread over great distances and connect distant people. In the preceding chapters we discussed research indicating that cheaper and more widespread physical, imaginative and communicative travel makes social networks less dense, more far-flung and mobile. While it is clearly plausible to claim that travel distances between members of networks have increased in the latter part of the twentieth century, neither transport research nor social science research have systematically measured or mapped distances between members of networks and associated networking practices, now or in the past. In this chapter we attempt to rectify this by examining to what degree weak and strong ties are spatially distributed and sustained through specific geographies of travel, meetings and communications. We examine the time–space structures of social networks and the mobilities of travel, talk and text flowing between each respondent and his/her strong ties.

First, we examine the respondents' residential mobility over the last 15 years. How often, how far and for what reasons have they moved? Second, we employ methods that can measure how geographically dispersed their networks are. We measure how far they live from their significant others. Then we examine if and how distance influences the practices of phoning, texting, emailing and meeting up. Does distance matter? Third, we map and examine individual networks that possess characteristics that are typical or likely to be so in the future, and we use the qualitative interview material to develop cultural landscapes to contextualize these network geographies (for a shortened and more qualitative account, see Larsen, Axhausen and Urry 2006).

Residential Mobility

Each respondent has on average moved to a different town or city 2.3 times in the past 15 years. 43 per cent lived outside the North-West of England when commencing primary school; 70 per cent once lived outside this region; two-fifths worked or studied abroad for a few months at the minimum. The majority have thus experiences of living in different places beyond the North-West of England. Yet two-fifths now live in the same town or place where they started primary school. However, only one has never lived in another place, so the rest have returned to their hometown at some point. So, rather than being immobilized by their hometown, people have returned home after years of living elsewhere. This is interestingly consistent with Doyle and Nathan's finding (2001; and see Chapter 4 above) that around 45 per cent of the UK population lives and works within five miles of where they were born. Exploring residential biographies over time thus highlight how we should be careful with making clear-cut distinctions between those deemed 'immobile' and those 'mobile'.

Much residential mobility is related to career moves and especially higher education, which also accounts for why the 13 respondents who attended university (mainly the architects) have moved most and over the longest distances. Architectural students are extraordinarily mobile: only two of the architects in our sample studied at a university in their hometown and the others moved some 208 km within the UK when they began Part 1 of their studies; some took Part 2 at another university and the obligatory year out practice training somewhere else again (in some cases this was near their parents because of free accommodation) during the five years it takes to become a fully qualified architect. Four studied for some months abroad. The reasons for studying elsewhere were not only academic but had also to do with 'escaping' parents and experiencing new places and people.

By contrast, respondents without university degrees have made fewer long-distance moves. However, there are important exceptions. One male, now a well-paid sales manager, substituted provincial Warrington with metropolitan Manchester to fulfil his ambitions (29 km). Two fitness instructors worked on a Caribbean cruise ship (where they eventually fell in love with each other), to experience the world and take advantage of the fact that they had few obligations to others. As one of them says:

> ... I always regretted not getting an opportunity to travel. And when my relationship split up, the job that I was in didn't have huge career prospects, it was basically a nine to five job. So I then had an option ... thought well I've not got a house, not got a relationship, [or] a career, if I'm ever going to do it, now is the time to do it. So I went off there with the plan of spending three or four years working for this agency. I ended up in the Caribbean. (No. 16, male fitness manager, mid-thirties)

Similar to Mason's findings (2004b), when our interviewees talk about residential mobility they refer to relationships (or lack of), commitments to friends, parents and especially partners. They are reflexively aware that their mobility has effects upon their immediate network, and this sometimes delays and discourages them from moving. This is how the sales manager mentioned above puts it:

> ... I'm very career focused ... Warrington is a town mentality. I originally moved to live with one of my friends in Manchester. ... That was quite difficult to make that move because my dad had passed away and my mum was becoming more reliant on me being there. So, although there was never a great time to do it, it was something that I had to do ... I mean I didn't move out until I was 20, so it was two years after I was ready to move out, but I had to ... grievous time. (No. 14, male sales manager, mid-twenties)

This also means that some people end up living in places more or less against their will. Some respondents live in the North-West of England only because their partner strongly desires to live there or refuses to move elsewhere. A receptionist and a sales adviser reflect upon why they happen to be in Manchester:

> I came to live here with my boyfriend after he finished university. I finished the year before he did ... I'm from Devon and he's from Northampton but we met at university in Oxford and then we came up here because he's got friends in Manchester ... He met them at school, Northampton, but they were at university in Manchester and are still here. (No. 12, female receptionist, early twenties)

> Well when I moved to London, I said to my girlfriend: 'let's try and make a go of it in London, and we'd spend say a year here and see how it goes'. So we spent a year in London, unhappy, and I think the whole of the time she wasn't completely happy. There was something there that wasn't happy, and previously she'd lived in Manchester. And she has got a lot of friends in Manchester and she didn't have many friends in London. So the main focus behind it was I promised her that we'd try it for a year in London, and then if it's not happy enough, we'll move to Manchester and try and live in Manchester ... I moved up here for her. And she's a lot happier. You know, I haven't lived in Manchester before so it's a complete new beginning for me. I haven't got any friends up here, but obviously I go out with her friends, and obviously getting new social groups. From my point of view, because I haven't got any friends, it has been hard. (No. 10, male sales adviser, late twenties)

These people's residential biographies are thus relational, shaped and negotiated with significant others. In a discussion about future plans, one architect highlights that this is a collective rather than an individual decision:

> We are at the position ... and I do say 'we' because I'm married and we have been together a long time, we are a unit ... we're in a good position where we don't have any ties at the moment. We don't have any children, we don't even own a house. And our ambitions are to go somewhere else and experience more. (No. 8, male architect, mid-twenties)

In Chapter 2 we discussed Kennedy's studies (2004, 2005) of cosmopolitan architects that move from city to city, from project to project, apparently unhindered by relationships and obligations other than those of work and personal ambition. In our study, the architects specifically describe obligations to significant others and their ambitions for family life: 'The older you get, the more commitments you have, the more difficult it is to do things like that. But if I was straight out of university, I could have gone anywhere, like London, Switzerland, France, Canada' (No. 7, male architect, late twenties). While they were highly mobile as students their careers have so far been less mobile; all of them have worked for the same practice for three to four years and only one has moved to a new town because of work. Rather than moving to new cosmopolitan places, several talk about settling down and moving back to their or their partner's roots, sometimes because their partner desires this:

I will actually be very reluctant to leave [Liverpool] in particular because I suppose in a way I've formed my identity by being here away from my family, and because it's such a great vibrant city. [But] I know that my wife in particular wants to move away and move close to our roots [Shrewsbury]. And I think if we do have a family, it will be a lot easier for us with the family close to hand. (No. 3, male architect, early thirties)

This quote is typical as it highlights how most interviewees believe that they will move closer or stay close to their parents or parents-in-law when they start a family, because physical support especially will be much more frequent 'with the family close to hand'. While much emotional and economical caring can be carried out at-a-distance through phone calls, emails and post, there is no (regular) help with cleaning, shopping and not least babysitting from family members if they are too distant. A female architect, who studied in Manchester and moved straight back to Liverpool to her family network after graduation, explains how she as a child 'suffered' from her parent's residential movement and stretched out social network. Her main ambition is to live in close proximity with her family and in-laws in Liverpool so that they can be fully involved with her future children:

... my parents both lived in Pudsey near Leeds. My mum went to London to university, my dad went to Lancaster and then to Liverpool for his masters. My mum moved to Liverpool and then got married, so we didn't live in the same city as my grandparents. And I never really knew them. I did know them because I saw them but I didn't know they didn't pick me up from school or I didn't go round for tea. We would go and visit them as a family, but ... I'd quite like [partner's] parents and my parents to be involved in my children being brought up ... John's parents live in Liverpool and so do mine. I'd be very reluctant to leave [Liverpool] because of that ... I've made the decision now that I want to stay in Liverpool near my family, near the clubs that I'm a member of. And I enjoy working here and they're my priorities, not work. (No. 1, female architect, early thirties)

Distances to Significant Others

We now analyse how far the respondents live from various categories of significant others as reported in Tables 7 and 8 in Appendix A.[1] The distances are great circle

---

1 The distribution of the distances gives a first impression of the spatial spread of the social networks. Still, the distances ignore the relative distribution in space. One can observe the same mean distance independently of the fact, whether the contacts are all clustered in one location or spread over many different locations in all compass directions. If one wants to account for this spread one needs to apply measures which capture the size of this social network geography. Schönfelder and Axhausen (2003) have solved the structurally identical problem of local activity spaces, i.e. the locations visited by same traveller over multiple weeks, by adapting and developing suitable measures. The simplest measure, the size of 95% confidence ellipse, has performed well and correlates highly with more sophisticated approaches (the confidence ellipse is the two-dimensional generalization of the more familiar confidence interval) (Schönfelder and Axhausen 2004; Vaze, Schönfelder and Axhausen 2005).

distances, so the actual distances travelled by car and train will be longer. The distances are summarized in Table 2 below.

We start by examining the geographies of the respondents' 'non-local friends'. Respondents listed up to 10 places (other than their own place of residence) where they have friends and we subsequently measured the distance between the respondent and each of these 'non-local friends'.

Table 2   Distance to categories of significant others (kilometres)

Categories of significant others	Min.	25 Percentile	Median	Mean	75 Percentile	Max.
Non-local friends	1	75	249	1398	595	18625
Close family members	0	0	59	693	203	9941
Most important people	0	0	26	395	117	16997

The first point to note is that their 'non-local friends' are widely scattered; they only have one 'non-local friend' in the north-west region on average and the average distance between them and their 'non-local friends' is a striking 1,398 km. All respondents have 'non-local friends', the mean being 6.5 (see Table 7 in Appendix A) (some had more than one friend in each place). Three could have listed more than 10 such places. Only five do not have friends in the UK more than 100 km away. They have friends in two foreign countries on average and 13 have friends in non-European countries. The three migrants have Russian (No. 2), South African (No. 24) and Irish (No. 5) friends back 'home' as well as across the UK and Europe. Several of the university graduates made friendships while studying abroad or with exchange students; some met English and foreign friends when working or travelling abroad (Nos 16 and 18); and some made English friends while touring the world (Nos 14, 22 and 23) or working abroad. Most of their friends in foreign countries are from back home rather than being from outside the UK (see Table 8 in Appendix A).

The architects are those with most 'non-local friends', both abroad and especially across the UK. Some non-architects have friends in Australia, America, New Zealand, Tanzania, Canada and Cape Town combined with few 'non-local friends' in England, which make the mean distance very high. The five people without friends more than 100 km away have not studied at universities, while all university graduates[2] have such distant friends across the UK. With a few exceptions the architects report that they have close university friends despite moving to different places during or after the course. So amongst these people many of the 'non-local friends' reported in Appendix A are old university friends.

---

2   In addition to the architects, interviewee Nos 10 (sales adviser), 11 (sales adviser) and 12 (receptionist) have university degrees.

Table 2 (and Tables 7 and 8 in Appendix A) also shows how close the respondents live to their parents, brothers and sisters, as well as other 'close family members' if the respondents state that they are of great significance to them.[3] Again we see striking distances between network members, the mean here being 693 km. Even when excluding the longest distances, the distance is still a considerable 251 km, so the respondents live far away from their 'close family members'. Indeed there are almost as many family ties abroad as within the respondents' immediate neighbourhood. Ten of them have 'close family members' abroad, so it is not only the three immigrants that have close family ties living abroad. Seven of the respondents have family networks that are exclusively located within the North-West of England, and only two of these family networks are nearby. The respondents have to journey to another city or town when meeting up with three out of four of their family members. These families do not live in Wellman's 'little boxes' (see Chapter 2) and extensive travel to meet up with their nearest family is unavoidable and almost always necessary.

We also asked the respondents to identify the locations of those people (up to 10) that they consider 'most important' to their present life and where they now live. Table 2 above summarizes the interviewees' distances to these people (see also Appendix A). Here one would expect the mean distance to be lower than with 'non-local friends' and 'close family members' as these people are strong ties. However, this is only partly the case. The people that the respondents are closest to and most dependent upon live in fact on average 395 km away from them.[4] A third have 'most important people' living abroad; 6 per cent living more than 1,000 km away; 7 per cent live more than 500 km away; 31 per cent live more than 100 km away; and 42 per cent live more than 50 km away.

This data supplements much of the literature reported in Chapter 2 highlighting how strong ties of care, support and affection are often dispersed. However, not all ties are dispersed. Indeed it seems that most respondents demonstrate a combination of far *and* nearby ties. No respondent has only distant ties. Table 7 in Appendix A show that the average distance to their three most nearby 'most important people' is 15 km and half of them live within a distance of 25 km. About half possess three such ties in the place where they live. Strong ties are not just to contacts far away (see also Appendix B).

We may indeed suggest that it is unsatisfactory for people to only have distant ties because it is difficult to meet such people impromptu for tea, beer, a football match or film. Indeed the interviews highlight the significance of local networking

---

3   The table only measures distances *between* cities/towns and not areas with cities/towns. All distances within cities/areas are therefore set at 0 km, even though distances between places in Liverpool and Manchester can be considerable. The table does not indicate 'local' distances and the averages underestimate the distances that separate people.

4   Unfortunately, two of the respondents (Nos 2 and 22) did not return this questionnaire. The reported figure would probably have been a little higher if we had the data for these two as their distances to 'non-local friends' and 'close family members' seem to be above average.

events to make and develop friends. One architect with a strongly dispersed social network joined the civic organization Round Table (www.roundtable.co.uk):

> … because we're quite new to the city in terms of the circle of friends that we have within the city. … And we just want to increase the opportunity to meeting … getting new friends, because … we wouldn't just go out to a pub on a Thursday night and start talking to people, we don't really do that. So we need to be in an environment where we're getting the opportunity to meet new folks, and this is kind of an organized way of doing that. (No. 5, male architect, mid-twenties)[5]

With a few exceptions these respondents do not have virtual friends. One exception is the Russian architect (No. 2) who regularly meets up with migrated Russians in chat rooms, and she has developed close friendships with a few of them even though they have never met physically. Even though many of their friendships are stretched out and much communicative travel in between meetings sustains them, few talked about friendships that occurred without intermittent co-presence.[6] Most interviewees agree with this statement:

> It is easier to keep in contact with people with text messages and emails. You can have a broader range of friends and it doesn't matter where they are in theory. [Yet] I don't think that good friendship is as good only via a message. That's not a proper friendship really. … I couldn't really stay friends with somebody if I am just messaging them and never seeing them. I would have to see them now and again in the flesh and do things … (No. 7, male architect, late twenties)

So we might say that as a rule strong ties – at least amongst reasonably prosperous people in the Western world – depends upon occasional co-presence, and too much distance can therefore be a problem. The respondents meet up with each of their 'most important people' every fourth day or so on average, but the frequency is largely determined by how far they live from each other (see Figure 1 and Figure 2 below).

But strong ties also depend upon communications. Each of the respondents have regular communications with each of their identified 'most important people', whether

---

5   This illustrates Watters's point that Putnam is wrong when he makes a clear-cut distinction between civic work and 'schmoozing' since so-called civic meetings are not only concerned with altruistic, civic matters but also with networking and forming and maintaining friendships (2004; and see Chapter 3).

6   Indeed they spelled out how strong ties become weak if sporadic emailing and texting now is the only foundation:

> I had a friend when I was at art school many years ago … and I've probably bumped into him once, and yet because he's a Manchester United fan, as soon as we got beaten the other night against Burnley, I had an email from him straight away the following morning, and generally that is our only contact. It's this kind of relationship … which is just over the internet or email rather than personal contact. And so he'll be sending me some kind of wind up message about Liverpool being out of the FA Cup and I'll send him one back saying well maybe you're not so good after all, you've got to play it tonight. (No. 3, male architect, early thirties)

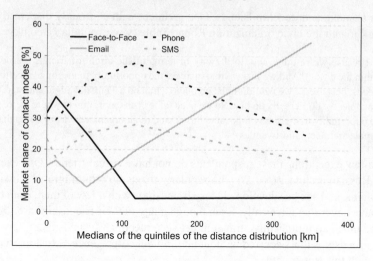

Figure 1   Shares of the modes of interaction over distance (%)

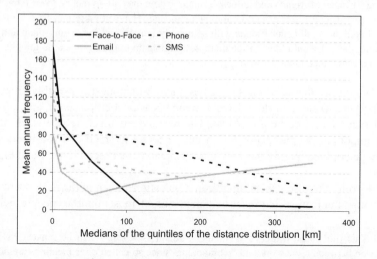

**Figure 2   Frequency of interaction over distance by mode of interaction
              (%)**

by email or phone or text message (but not necessarily all three). The respondents
talk every other day on the phone or text or email with their 'most important people'
on average, so they have more frequent interaction with them at-a-distance than
face-to-face (see Figure 1 and Figure 2 below). In-between physical meetings, they
overcome the 'frictions of distance' and manage dispersed networks by 'inhabiting'
'phone spaces' and the internet where connections are made in 'timeless' fashion.
Communication technologies free up time for socializing because people can be

in two places simultaneously and therefore can occasionally avoid time-consuming travel.

This communication is partly about coordinating meetings (see Chapter 7) and partly about ensuring communicative co-presence when physical meetings are impossible. Indeed all respondents agree that communications ease the 'pain' of being separated by distance: 'It's never really been a big problem. I know some people come to uni and they hate it because they're not near their family, whereas I speak to my dad every other day, I speak to my mum every other day' (No. 22, doorman, early twenties).

As the Russian architect, with her family still in Russia, says:

Well my parents in fact, although they are furthest away from everyone else, but they are kind of my immediate circle, although they are far away. So it's my brother, my mum ... I phone them once a week at the weekend ... If I don't phone on Saturday, my dad starts to ... oh she's not phoning, what's going on ... I try to do it first thing on Saturday morning. I try to stick with routine. [We talk for] an hour easily. .... We talk about personal things. ..... She always thinks I'm ill because I'm sniffling. (No. 2, female architect, early thirties)

Measuring Meetings and Communications

In Chapter 4 we discussed research suggesting that there is a 'death of distance' because of cheaper and faster corporeal, virtual and communicative travel. Figures 1 and 2 show how the respondents' meetings, phone calls, emails and text messaging (SMS) are organized with their 'most important people' over distance. The distances were grouped into five classes with equal numbers of observations. For each of those quintiles the median distance was calculated to anchor the points on the graph.

These figures demonstrate that increasing distance between network members means less frequent face-to-face contact. With increasing distance there is declining frequency of those face-to-face meetings. The respondents socialize with their local most significant people every other day or so; those living up to 30 km away every fourth day or so; those living 30–80 km away almost once a week. However, they meet with those living 400 km away as often as with those living 125 km away. So while distant ties are less likely to meet up, they do so intermittently; no matter the cost. The figures show that strong ties cannot sustain themselves without occasional physical co-presence.

Indeed the respondents meet all their 'most important people' at least once a year. Yet if people live too far from their most significant network members their social capital will diminish. This perhaps explains the significance of local networking events and why all respondents have some of their 'most important people' within their immediate environment, even if they have only moved there recently.

Figures 1 and 2 also illustrate that phone calls (both landline and mobile) decline when distance increases. As discussed in Chapter 2, most phone calls are brief local calls concerned with coordination (Geser 2004; and see Chapter 8). The respondents call their local 'most important people' almost every other day, which is more or less as often as they meet up. Long-distance calls are less frequent because they are more expensive per minute (especially international calls) and distant ties meet less frequently, so there is less need for coordination. While phone calls travel well, in practice they do not travel long (the timeless travel of telephony does yet come free for most, although internet-based NetMeeting and especially voice-over-IP telephony is in the process of changing this). Nonetheless, among distant ties phone calls are pivotal and they often substitute for face-to-face meetings when these cannot take place. The respondents phone their most distant ties much more often that they meet up face-to-face, every second or third week compared with every second or third month. And they speak on the phone with those living 80–250 km away 10 times as often as they meet up. These figures indicate that phone calls to some extent overcome the friction of distance and substitute for physical meetings.

Figures 1 and 2 also show that respondents text those close-by the most. Those in the nearby environment are likely to receive one or more texts every third day or so while those living more than 250 km away receive text messages once or twice a month. This decay with distance resembles the figures for face-to-face meetings and especially phone calls. In addition to gossiping, SMS texting is intricately tied up with the complex micro-geographies of coordinating and accessing meetings (see Chapter 8).

But significantly the rate of emails increases with distance. Emails travel 'further' than phone calls and text messages. While emails are used least often to communicate with ties around the corner, the respondents email those living more than 250 km away almost every week, and this is more often than with any of the others, except local ties (coordination emails). Around a half of all interactions with most distant ties are through email. So it is primarily email that ensures that regular contact is sustained in long periods of little or no face-to-face interactions. Emails travel extremely fast and cheaply over great distances. Whereas distance matters in relation to face-to-face meetings (price and time) phone calls (price) and text messages (price), emails are indifferent to distances, both in terms of price and speed. Greetings, jokes, invitations, photographs and so on reach any distance within seconds when flying *timeless class* with email, and this first-class service comes free (once broadbanded) on the internet. These figures suggest that email substitutes for expensive long distance calls in periods where face-to-face meetings are impossible due to travel time and price. Thus those without proper access to, or skills to use the Internet, have less contact with distant ties.

Distance is also a matter of how long a contact has existed. Table 3 shows that the more recent the 'most important people', the closer they live to the current address of the interviewees. In the lowest quartile of distances 55.6 per cent of the contacts are less than seven years old, while in the highest quartile this share is only around one-third.

Table 3   Duration of 'most important people' and distances from respondents

		Distance in km banded as quartiles			
		0	*0.1–15.4*	*15.5–114.8*	*114.9 +*
Duration	0–7 years (%)	55.6	57.9	45.0	32.0
	8–33 years (%)	44.4	42.1	55.0	68.0

Geography – distance and proximity – matters greatly in relation to weak or new ties but apparently less so with 'strong ties'. Old and rooted ties have more foundation to exist at-a-distance. While some ties have much endurance, networks are on the move partly because residential time–space biographies are uneven through time (Pred, 1977).

In this chapter we have documented how most of the respondents' social networks are widely dispersed. Yet even dispersed networks consist of nearby ties, so the common distinction between far and nearby ties is too simple. Then we documented how there is a friction of distance in relation to face-to-face meetings but not so with email. The analysis demonstrates that distance matters; too much distance to various categories of significant others will have detrimental effects upon one's social capital. Network capital is a relational outcome that also depends upon other peoples' location and mobility.

Mapping Individual Networks

In the rest of this chapter we examine these general findings in relation to individual networks by describing the networking practices of four typical respondents, illustrated by some novel map-making techniques developed for this project. We visualize in all cases the complex local, national and global linkages, obligations and interdependent mobilities that make up these four social networks. Each brings out how contemporary social networks possess complex geographies of nearby and faraway ties and how the friction of distance is lived with in practice. These are Maps 1–4, in the colour section.

Map 1 (No. 21, Male University Porter, Mid-twenties)

On the face of it this person's network resembles a little box in that his national ties are exclusively located in a relatively small area of the North-West of England, stretching from Carnforth to Morecambe (8 km), to Lancaster (1.4 km), to Preston (34 km) and to Southport (45 km). The two main hubs are his hometown Morecambe and Preston where the majority of his 'most important people' live, and, as the boxes reveal, these are predominantly family members. His wife is from Southport and her brother is one his 'most important people'. So while his 'most important people' by today's standards are fairly close by, they are not exclusively local. The average distance to them is 19 km and this is the second shortest average among the respondents. His 'little box' is thus beyond walking distance and depends upon much regional travel.

This pattern partly reflects this person's limited residential mobility. As a child and young teenager he lived for 10 years in Northwich with his parents (92 km from Morecambe) before jointly moving back to Morecambe. He has subsequently moved residence several times, but always within Morecambe, because this is where his family is, where he feels at home and housing is affordable compared with surrounding towns and cities. However, he almost moved to Southport when moving together with his partner who is equally attached to her hometown Southport:

> The general idea was … to get a house down there, and then it proved too expensive … so we ended up moving up here. … It was either always Southport or Morecambe, because … we're very close with our families so we didn't want to move too far away from either of them. (No. 21, male porter, mid-twenties)

So it was a contest only between Southport and Morecambe. Yet the little box nature of his network is thus not entirely of his own making, as Southport proved too expensive for their relatively low incomes.

The boxes on Map 1 reveal that respondent No. 21 engages in much face-to-face interaction with his significant others. The two people he sees most often – respectively everyday and every other day – live around the corner in Morecambe and within walking distance. Yet also, despite a 45- or 60-km car journey, he sees his brother-in-law weekly and his cousin fortnightly, either in Southport/Preston or Morecambe. This is possible since he has his own car (one indication of network capital) that his father gave to him when purchasing a new one. This example illustrates how cars are crucial in making little worlds bigger and in enabling regular face-to-face meetings between people that live in other regional towns or cities.

The boxes also show that he has little communicative proximity, whether through phoning, texting or email. The people that he sees most are also the people that he phones and text most, which indicates that many of his calls are for brief coordination (Geser 2004; and see Chapter 8). Despite having access to the internet at work (not a private work email), he does not email any of his 'most important people' as none of them email regularly. This also illustrates how network capital is relational since email access is worthless if one's network members lack or reject this form of network capital. He is forced to call or text with his ties.

However, the global map shows that he has friends and family members living abroad and email is crucial in connecting easily and cheaply:

> I've got an uncle who lives in America so I email him a lot because it's a lot cheaper than phone calls. [I have friends from] Preston, that now live in … Nice. So they send an email once a month. They send it to all their friends … say 30/50 people. That's the only other email I get as well. (No. 21, male porter, mid-twenties)

Email for him is a technology of long-distance communication with people that have left 'home'. This example illustrates how people with otherwise relative little box networks often possess a few far-flung connections that they predominantly stay in contact with through email. Yet his relationship to his uncle in the USA is also sustained through visits and physical travel as the uncle regularly visits England and occasionally offers a ticket to the USA (see Chapter 7).

Most literature reviewed in Chapter 2 discusses mobile networks in relation to people who are themselves mobile, but this ignores how the less mobile can be much affected by the more mobile and their extensive network capital. This respondent's international ties are not a product of his mobility; he is rather affected by the mobility of others. His networks would have been less dispersed if *they* had stayed put. As a general point this example helps us to grasp how dispersed networks do not need to be of one's own making, because networks are relational. Most networks will consist of a combination of very mobile and less mobile people, and mobile, far-flung networks are thus not only common amongst the privileged few.

Map 2 (No. 18, Female Personal Trainer, Mid-thirties)

Map 2 highlights how long-distance communicative travel is habitually part of some people's network practices and how email and phoning can sustain and develop ties formed through physical travel.

One striking feature of this map is that three of her identified 'most important people' live in the USA. Even more striking, as the boxes reveal, are the weekly emails and phone calls flowing between Manchester and the USA. She makes expensive international calls at home and emails at the local library since she has no access to email at work or home. These strong ties, which have lasted up to 15 years, are almost exclusively sustained through communication at-a-distance, as they meet up only once a year at most (flight tickets alone cost around £400; her annual salary is £18,000).

Their weekly communication helps her and her friends to overcome the distance separating them:

> I can call these guys any time and we just talk for hours and it's like I saw them yesterday. It's really strange, because I even said to Sarah yesterday, you just sound like you're in the next room. She just sounded like she was next door to me. Lou phoned first from Chicago and then Mia phoned in the afternoon from New York, and wished me happy birthday which was really really nice. We always send birthday cards, emails and speaking on the telephone … just to say hello, how are you, we're doing really well, what they've been up to, what the boys are doing at school and just how things are going in life in general really. Because Sarah is having her kitchen refurbished, so that's a topic of conversation. (No. 18, female personal trainer, mid-thirties)

Hour-long conversations and letter-type emails resemble face-to-face conversations in enabling people to catch up, fulfil social obligations (for example, saying 'happy birthday'), discuss personal problems, share gossip and so on. And occasionally they do meet up, once a year if money and time allow it, or at a special event that makes it more or less obligatory. In the next chapter we see how a wedding will next bring them all together.

So how did they meet? The international ties map shows that this person has lived in the USA. In 1991, while working as an au pair for a year in Connecticut she met Sarah[7] and at a subsequent tourist-type visit she introduces her to Lou. Between 1995 and 2000 she works as a personal trainer on a cruise ship in the Caribbean and here she meets her third American friend. Her two 'most important people' – best friend and co-residing partner – locally in Manchester are people she also met on this cruise ship. So, as she says: 'most of my really good friends, I have either met whilst I have been travelling abroad or I've met them on the cruise ship'. In contrast to the respondent behind Map 1, her mobile, dispersed network is very much of her own making.

This map illustrates how periods of travelling, working or studying abroad normally have lasting network effects especially now that travel and long-distance communications are widespread. In Chapter 2 we discussed how sociologists like Beck-Gernsheim argue that 'individualization' and mobility mean that relationships are short lived, so our age is one of 'more beginnings' and 'farewells'. However, this tends to overlook the increasing significance of *reunions* within relationships conducted at-a-distance (2002, 41; and see Chapter 2). In other words, more farewells are not necessarily the same as a refusal of permanent ties.

This map neatly illustrates how most social networks are made up of close-by and faraway ties, face-to-face sociability and mediated talk. Except for her American friends and a friend in London, all this respondent's ties are within North-West England, in Manchester and her old hometown Chester, where her parents, sisters and other friends live. While they text or phone a lot, it is these people that provide her with vital doses of physical co-presence. Respondent No. 18 has access to a car on a daily basis and travels the 56 km to Chester once every week. She would prefer to live in Chester but it is too expensive so she settled in Manchester. She is particularly keen to move back in the near future as she hopes start a family, and her family's physical support is believed to be crucial. Being on the move is no longer so desirable for this respondent, yet her social network is likely to remain dispersed because she keeps her distant ties alive mainly through communicative travel and very occasional tourist-type meetings.

Dispersed networks sustained primarily through communicative travel are likely to be even more significant in the future where broadbanded internet and especially free telephony on the internet (as now with Skype) will make it much cheaper and easier. However, this research suggests that rather than substituting meetings and travel, free communicative travel is likely to increase it, because with cost-free communication, ties are less likely to weaken when they become dispersed and this creates the need for intermittent physical travel.

---

7   The names in this section are fictitious.

Map 3 (No. 24, Male Doorman, Mid-thirties)

In Chapters 2 to 4 we briefly discussed how the number of international migrants has increased since the 1960s, and that this potentially produces mobile, dispersed networks that depend upon much imaginative and corporeal travel (VFR tourism) to sustain ties to places and people back home.

Map 3 visualizes one example of a migration network: respondent No. 24, who now lives in Thornton having moved to South Africa as a young schoolboy with his family. Some 10 years ago, he and his partner (born and raised in South Africa by English parents), decide to 'return', believing that Britain offers a better life than post-apartheid South Africa. They moved to Bristol (and not any other town) because his sister had recently moved there from South Africa:

> My sister was living there at that particular time. I've only got one sister and she'd moved back to England about two years previous to us moving and she offered to help us with accommodation and setting us up and helping looking for work, etc. So that was my main reason because my sister was there. She was there purely for work. She had no family connections in Bristol either ... we did want to come back to the UK, but the actual city of Bristol, the only reason was because my sister was there. (No. 24, male porter, mid-thirties)

Additional motivation to make this difficult move was that his mother and some good friends had just made the same move; the mother moving back to her roots in North-West England while the friends went to London on a two-year tourist visa. This couple lived in Bristol for four years, before moving back to his roots in the North-West, triggered mainly by a job offer, but also of the idea of moving closer to his mother now back home. This case demonstrates how networks are implicated in both the timing and the routes and destinations that migrants follow.

This network illustrates how migration is not a single one-way journey from one home to another, but a more complex one involving regular communication and journeys to South Africa and South African friends located across the UK and elsewhere. His 'most important people' in London, Bournemouth, Stockholm and Canada are all old friends or family members from his time in South Africa or to a lesser extent are South Africans that he has been introduced to while living in the UK (the friends in Bournemouth). This illustrates how migration networks are often spread across multiple places and how migrants sustain close ties with people from back home, whether they are still at home or also on the move. Most of his strong ties are thus long-lasting friendships, and he argues that such 'deep-rooted' friendships can stand the test of distance:

> They are very deep-rooted friendship, which is long lasting, and I don't think will ever go away. I think if you've made a friend just recently, that time you've been friends you will soon forget about them ... if you've got experience of growing up with them and been through a lot of things, then I think that strengthens a friendship definitely. (No. 24, male porter, mid-thirties)

Here he also refers to the fact that he has more or less lost contact with the friends that he briefly knew in Bristol.

The major reason that this dispersed transnational network can sustain itself is that it occasionally meets up, individually but also collectively, which is something that the migration literature has largely overlooked until recently. That network geographies like his are more and more widespread and this explains why VFR tourism has grown so rapidly.

One important meeting-place is his friend's home in London where his friends from Bournemouth and Sweden are likely to show up too when travelling there every half-year or so:

> The friend in Sweden is also a best friend from Cape Town who's now living there. He also flies to London. Their brother is actually my best friend in London; he's the brother of the one in Sweden. So if we go to London we may get to see him there as well as the Bournemouth crowd. (No. 24, male porter, mid-thirties)

Respondent No. 24 normally travels the 381 km to London by car because it is cheaper when travelling with his family and because he can make a detour to his sister's home or Bournemouth. Another meeting-place is Cape Town where they try to meet up each summer. Here the flight tickets alone cost around £700, which represents a major obstacle and this prevents him and his family travelling every year (despite free accommodation). Possibilities for cheap, flexible long-distance travel are thus essential for his network capital (as we will discuss in detail in Chapter 7), as VFR tourism is essential for his social life.

By contrast with respondent No. 18 and her American friends (Map 2), this network is sustained primarily through corporeal travel. This respondent phones and emails very little, approximately once a month on average with each tie. He thinks that it is very expensive to call South Africa (his father is the only one that he phones regularly), and it is too expensive for his friends in South Africa to email him. This network's emails are different from respondent No. 18. Rather than personal letter-type emails theirs are collectively distributed jokes. They are nonetheless meaningful as they distribute commonality and connectivity at the same time as amusement:

> [Some days] ago I received an email from South Africa from one of my close male friends … just a funny joke … Even though some of these are general and you're just on the address list, you know it's from a good friend, so even though the friend doesn't particularly go to you: 'how are you', you still get a feeling that that friendship is there because of who's it from, you know, and because they have obviously got the same sense of humour as you. The sender will obviously know that you will find it funny. So there's that connection there. (No. 24, male porter, mid-thirties)

While many of his 'most important people' are very dispersed indeed, Map 3 also reveals that three of his 'most important people' are local: his mother, a very recent workmate and a friend without connection to South Africa. Clearly, especially given his thoughts on the different significances of old friends *contra* new friends, he

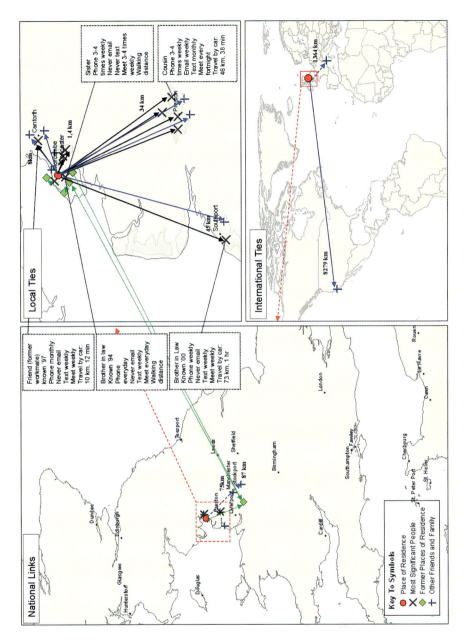

Map 1   Respondent 21

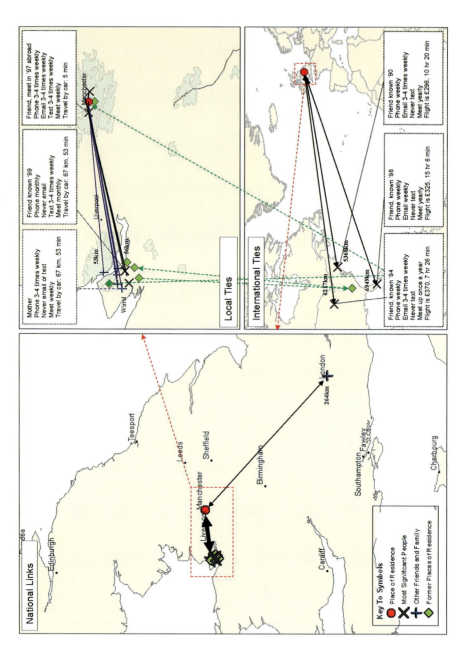

National Links

Local Ties

International Ties

Mother.
Phone 3-4 times weekly
Never email or text
Meet weekly
Travel by car: 67 km, 53 min

Friend known '99
Phone monthly
Never email
Text 3-4 times weekly
Meet monthly
Travel by car: 67 km, 53 min

Friend, meet in '97 abroad
Phone 3-4 times weekly
Email 3-4 times weekly
Text 3-4 times weekly
Meet weekly
Travel by car: 5 min

Friend known '90
Phone weekly
Email 3-4 times weekly
Never text
Meet yearly
Flight is £296, 10 hr 20 min

Friend, known '98
Phone weekly
Email weekly
Never text
Meet yearly
Flight is £325, 15 hr 6 min

Friend, known '94
Phone weekly
Email 3-4 times weekly
Never text
Meet up once a year
Flight is £370, 7 hr 26 min

Key To Symbols

● Place of Residence
✕ Most Significant People
✚ Other Friends and Family
◆ Former Places of Residence

Map 2   Respondent 18

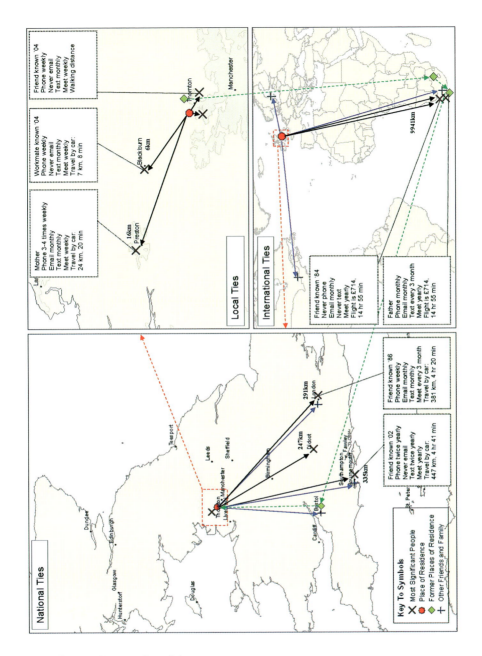

Map 3   Respondent 24

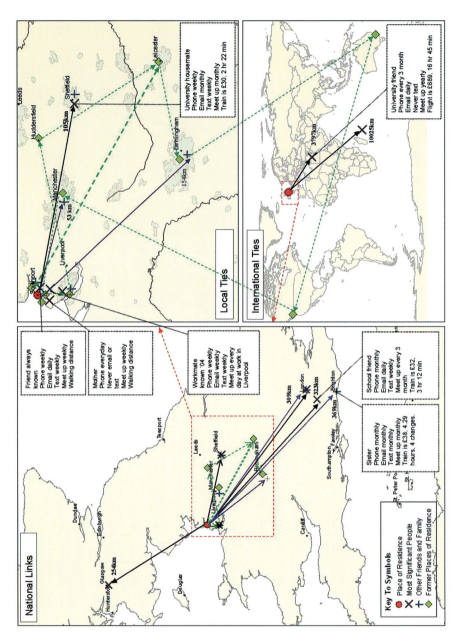

National Links

Friend always
known
Phone weekly
Email daily
Text weekly
Meet up weekly
Walking distance

Mother
Phone everyday
Never email or
text
Meet up weekly
Walking distance

Workmate
known '04
Phone weekly
Email weekly
Text weekly
Meet up every
day at work in
Liverpool

Sister
Phone monthly
Email monthly
Text monthly
Meet up monthly
Train is £38, 4.29
hours, 4 changes.

School friend
Phone monthly
Email daily
Text weekly
Meet up every 3
month
Train is £32,
3 hr 12 min

309km
323km
369km
254km

Leeds
Sheffield
Manchester
Liverpool
Birmingham
London
Brighton
Southampton Fawley
St. Peter Po
Cardiff
Glasgow
Hunterston
Douglas
Edinburgh
Dundee
Newport

Local Ties

Leeds
Huddersfield
Manchester
Liverpool
Sheffield
Leicester
Birmingham
Stockport

105km
53 km
154km

University housemate
Phone weekly
Email monthly
Text weekly
Meet up monthly
Train is £30, 2 hr 22 min

International Ties

University friend
Phone every 3 month
Email daily
Never text
Meet up yearly
Flight is £689, 16 hr 45 min

3797km
10025km

Key To Symbols

● Place of Residence
✕ Most Significant People
✚ Other Significant People
◆ Former Places of Residence

Map 4   Respondent 4

cannot be as close to these new friends as to his old South Africans, but they are very important to his present everyday as they are a 'bridge' to his new home and people that it only takes a short walk or drive to socialize with. This example illustrates how strong ties in practice may often be what we would otherwise classify as weak ties. The distinction between weak ties and strong ties are often blurred as they depend upon people's network geographies. For newcomers, weak ties can quickly turn into strong ties and they can equally quickly become weak again, if one of them moves on.

Map 4 (No. 4, Male Architect, Early Thirties)

Map 4 illustrates how widespread residential mobility often will result in dispersed networks and much weekend travel, even if the person returns home. It also questions the idea that home is necessarily a place of attachment.

This respondent (No. 4) has also moved much and yet returned to his childhood city, to Southport. In between leaving in 1991 and returning in 2004, he lived in five places in the UK as well as spending shorter periods in Sydney and Vancouver. He very much expresses a mobile or cosmopolitan sensibility: 'I don't think it is healthy just to be in the one place all the time. I think it is healthy to get around and see what's going on in the rest of the world.'

We saw that respondents who went to university moved most often and over the longest distances; this architect was particular mobile as a student. He moved from Southport to Liverpool to go to technical college; to Huddersfield to take Part 1 of his architectural degree; back to his parents in Southport for his year out to work for a Liverpool based practice; to Leicester for Part 2 and Birmingham for Part 3. Then he travelled with his girlfriend, spending one year in Australia and Vancouver, working occasionally for an international architectural firm, mainly to cover his travel expenses: 'it was really more home-work experience than anything serious … just sort of subsistence living really'. It is well known that gap-year travel, which is increasingly common amongst youngish well-educated people, combines lively city life and work experience (Conradson and Latham 2005a).[8]

From here this respondent moved to Manchester because of a good job offer, while his girlfriend went back to Glasgow to pursue a career there, so a desire to pursue careers was one major reason that their relationship turned into a long-distance one. Partly because of this distance the relationship eventually broke up. And after a few years he moved back to Southport. That this cosmopolitan architect ends up in his hometown turns out to be an accidental homecoming that has little to do with place attachment and more with his career and getting on the property ladder:

---

8   Conradson and Latham (2005a) discuss how a vibrant cosmopolitan city like London attracts very large numbers of such youngish people from New Zealand, who normally stay for a couple of years before moving back to NZ to start family or a 'proper' career.

> Now I ultimately decided I'm going to work in Manchester and that's where I'm going to settle down … When I reached that level where I was looking to buy a flat, I was looking round and there was nowhere in Manchester that was [affordable]. … So I kind of bought a flat back in Southport, which was still quite cheap, and I thought well I'll rent that out. In the meantime I've got this job offer […] and they were desperate looking for people in Liverpool. So I thought right fine … it seems like an opportunity, I've got this flat, I suppose I can [live there]. … I'm here [Liverpool] now because it is one of the more exciting places to be as an architect. I think a lot of people might end up back where they lived because they've got nowhere else to go … I mean the only reason I do live here at the moment is because there's a massive project here, and if this massive project wasn't here, I wouldn't be here. (No. 4, male architect, early thirties)

While returning home, this respondent is likely to move elsewhere when his current project ends or a new one comes up. He is one of few respondents with little idea about where he will be living in five years' time and he can easily see himself living abroad. This architect thus shows some resemblance to the 'global architects' researched by Kennedy (2004, 2005).

Widespread residential mobility as a student and as aspiring architect, coupled with well-educated, mobile friends, explain why this respondent's network is widely dispersed across the UK and abroad (living on average 1,484 km from his 'most important people', see Table 8 in Appendix A) and he is a stranger in his old hometown, so he needs to rejuvenate or reform friendships there:

> Because I've done a lot of moving around in the last couple of years, I've got a lot of friends, contacts all over the place … even though I am here in the place where I started, I've gone full circle, I don't actually know that many people here and people I do know I don't want to know any more … all the friends I've … grown up with when I was in Southport, they are all spread out all over the country now and I'm still in touch with a lot of them … [However,] I can see myself being here [in Southport] for a few years at the moment, so I've kind of put down a few roots and stuff, but at the same time … (No. 4, male architect, early thirties)

His networking practices are thus a balance between meeting new people in Southport and Liverpool and sustaining old ties with friends living elsewhere through email and weekend travel.

He has already set down roots as his three of his identified 'most important people' are in Southport: his mother, an old friend and a very recent workmate. These are people that he meets regularly. But the other boxes on Map 4 reveal that he also has much interaction with his non-local friends. For example, he emails his old university friend in Mauritius daily and meets up with his sister monthly despite requiring a 4.5-hour train journey (involving four changes) costing at least £38. He receives and sends some 75 private emails weekly and undertook 27 longer weekend journeys to visit friends and family members in 2004 (see Table 4 in Chapter 7). And when he is not on the move visiting people he often spends his weekends hosting distant ties. His network capital is high as he has access to private email at work and a substantial budget for leisure travel (this is discussed in Chapters 7 and 8).

He illustrates how commitments and commitments to friends and family members have not dissolved in 'liquid modernity' (Bauman 2000a), even among very mobile people.

Conclusion

In this chapter we developed ways to measure and map networks and their associated networking practices. We began with documenting the scale of respondents' residential mobility over the last 10–15 years. It was shown that most have experiences of living beyond the North-West and this includes people that now live in their old hometown. We went on to measure the interviewees' distances to their significant others and it was shown that many such ties are strikingly distant, and this is so across the three occupations and industries sampled.

Much literature highlights that weak ties are becoming dispersed, while this research shows that this is also often the case with strong ties, or what we have called 'most important people'. Following Simmel, we may say that people often live with strangers nearby, while their significant others are far away. This indicates that 'time–space compression' has not compressed but *enlarged* social network geographies. Yet nearness also matters in relation to strong ties. None of the respondents has only distant 'most important people' and they stress the need for such ties locally. This suggests that social networks of 'strong ties' are a combination of distant *and* nearby ties. The interviewees' individual networks comprise complex geographies of close-by and distant ties, new and old ties as well as multiple places and 'homes'.

Nearby strong ties are crucial; we have documented that phone calls, texting and especially face-to-face meetings become less regular with increasing distances. The trend is reversed with email. This indicates that email in particular substitutes for face-to-face sociality when distance makes it too time-consuming and expensive. However, while the frequency of face-to-face meetings falls dramatically with increasing distances, *none* of the respondents have 'most important people' that are only sustained through communicative travel.

While it is difficult to make gender comparisons with this small sample, it was evident that women spend more time talking on the phone and are more likely to stress the importance of living close to other family members if they start having a family of their own.

We elaborated upon these quantitative findings by examining four instructive networks illustrated though novel maps showing the distribution of strong ties and mobility practices. These four illustrations showed that networks are distant for different reasons and sustained through various means. They also brought out how the common distinctions between mobile and immobile people, local and non-local networks are too simple and non-relational. The four respondents' networks are affected by the mobility of others in complex and contingent ways. Network geographies are not purely of one's own making as the individualization thesis argues. Less mobile people can in theory have very dispersed networks while this is not always the case here with those apparently more mobile.

In the following two chapters we develop further some of the findings of this chapter. In Chapter 7 we examine the social significance of long-distance travel in societies where distant ties are common, while Chapter 8 examines relationships between physical travel and communications through exploring how mobile communications can serve to coordinate a mobile social life.

Chapter 7

Travel and Meetings

Introduction

In the last chapter we documented the geographical spread of the reported social networks and how virtual, communicative and corporeal travel connects dispersed social relations. Chapters 2, 3 and 4 documented how it is that much leisure and tourist-type travel should not be seen as marginal, superfluous and by implication unnecessary. In this chapter we examine in detail the significance of corporeal or physical travel. We explore to what degree and how travel is used to network, to connect networks and meet up with distant connections through face-to-face proximities. The chapter thus examines whether physical mobility is not necessarily detrimental to social capital but can in fact produce this very valuable social good (for a condensed version of this analysis, see Larsen, Urry and Axhausen forthcoming).

We begin with documenting how many times in 2004 the respondents travelled within the UK and abroad, and we test our hypotheses (formulated in Chapter 5) regarding the uneven distribution of travel. Then, elaborating upon the fivefold schema in Chapter 4, we examine why people travel, and document the scale of VFR tourism. The rest of the chapter then analyses how the respondents visit and receive the hospitality of close friends, workmates and family members living elsewhere, and travel to fulfil social obligations by attending Christmas parties, birthdays, weddings, funerals and so on.

Travel Patterns

Table 4 shows that in 2004 respondents made on average 2.4 international leisure journeys and almost 10 UK leisure journeys of more than 100 miles. The average number of business trips made that year by these respondents was 0.2 abroad and 2.4 within the UK. 19 out of 24 travelled abroad for leisure at least once, while two went on an international business trip. We may thus say that these people travel more for life than for a living.

In Chapter 4 we showed that travel is unevenly distributed. In the sample, the three people making most long-distance UK trips undertook 27, 25 and 10 journeys respectively, while six of the sample made one or none. There are disparities between and within the three occupations. The nine architects undertook on average 3.1 international journeys and 15.6 domestic journeys. The figures for those in the fitness industry are 1.8 and 4.6, and for the security staff 1.8 and 6.4. As hypothesized, the architects travel significantly more than the two other subgroups. This is in part because they have higher incomes (see Table 4) and more distant connections resulting from their mobile university biographies. Practically all the architects have mobile travel biographies, which is another indicator of network capital.

The picture is less clear cut with regard to the two other subgroups. For instance, the two receptionists (Nos 12 and 13), who earn modest incomes (£15,000 and £13,000), make many long-distance journeys within the UK to visit friends and family members back home and university friends elsewhere, while the high-earning (£30,000) sales manager (No. 14) did not undertake any long-distance journeys within the UK because his social network is located within North-West England. But while the sales manager went abroad three times in 2004, the two receptionists only managed one such trip between them because of limited funds. The two people (Nos 19 and 24) that did not undertake any long-distance travel in 2004 have relatively low incomes (£16,000 and £14,000). Income is an important element of network capital but it does not determine travel behaviour. Rather appropriate income, network capital *and* distant connections generate leisurely travel and mobile biographies.

Why, then, do these people travel a lot? The aim of 45 per cent of international journeys is to visit other places. Visiting significant others and attending weddings, stag nights, funerals and reunions account for around one-third of the respondents' journeys abroad. This indicates that leisure travel is heterogeneous, as it comprises both the desire to visit exotic places and of networking with familiar faces, and these desires often coexist within the same journey. The remaining journeys are a hybrid of these two, and should not be forced into either category (common with closed questions using pre-coded purpose categories). Thus, overall, visiting what are seen as extraordinary places *and* meeting significant others often go hand in hand. As one respondent reported:

> It's usually a combination. Obviously with the cost of travelling and the cost of staying somewhere, if we can make the best out of the trip, the better. So if we can get in doing the tourist thing, doing the relaxation thing and doing the family thing all in one go, then that's convenient bonus. If my friend is in Berlin, then that's great because I've never been to Berlin before so I'm killing two birds with one stone. I'm looking forward to Berlin. (No. 10, male sales adviser, late twenties)

This last quotation illustrates how the term 'VFR tourism' is unsatisfactory because it underemphasizes the significance of specific places when visiting friends or family. In Chapter 3 we discussed how business travel often turns into leisure travel, and this is another way of 'killing two birds with one stone' that some of the respondents also demonstrate. Thus one explained:

> I'm canny basically on this. If I can, I'll find a reason to be down in London and I can get a ticket off work. It's an open ticket so I can use it whenever. ... So I can sort of like arrange a meeting on Friday, sorted. (No. 4, male architect, early thirties)

Table 4   **Long-distance journeys made by respondents**

No.	Occupation	Income	Long-distance journeys made in 2004	
			UK	Abroad
4	Architect	32,000	27	3
1	Architect	N/A	25	2
8	Architect	24,000	25	3
13	Receptionist	13,000	24	0
20	Porter	9,500	20	1
5	Architect	N/A	20	4
3	Architect	25,000	17	3
9	Architect	13,400	12	2
22	Doorman	11,000	10	2
10	Sales adviser	20,000	10	5
7	Architect	N/A	7	2
6	Architect	27,000	6	6
16	Fitness Instructor Manager	22,000	3	2
12	Receptionist	15,000	3	1
23	Doorman	15,000	3	4
22	Porter	12,455	3	3
18	Personal Trainer	18,000	2	2
24	Doorman	N/A	2	1
2	Architect	N/A	1	3
11	Sales adviser	20,000	0	4
14	Sales Manager	30,000	0	3
19	Porter	14,000	0	0
15	Sales Manager	19,000	0	2
17	Sales Staff	16,000	0	0
Average			9.7	2.4

Some explain that it is business travel that enables them to see their best friends. As this fitness instructor manager in Manchester says:

> My oldest and closest friend, this guy down in Oxford … We were as thick as thieves at school … We … lost contact for about a year … And it actually ended up that he came up for business to Bolton about two years ago, and he rang me and said 'I'm in Bolton, do you fancy meeting up?' … Now we probably meet up once every … every couple of months, that's probably as often as we meet up, just because his work is very hectic and so is mine, and also he's got a family and now I've got my fiancée. Most of the time it's

because work has taken us close to where we are. (No. 16, male fitness instructor, mid-thirties)

This illustrates how future travel surveys and tourist typologies need to be more complex in their categories in order to capture the ways in which many journeys serve several purposes and combine various modes of travel, hospitality and accomodation.

Travel theory and research have traditionally seen travellers as free-floating individuals seeking to maximize their 'pleasures'. They have often failed to notice the obligations that choreograph tourism escapes. In Chapter 3 we discussed how there are various more or less binding and more or less pleasurable obligations that require meetings of co-presence. There are obligations to places, objects, events and especially people. As a male architect says:

> The last [holiday] … was my mum's 60th birthday … we really couldn't afford it but we were keen to make it a special birthday for her so we got cheap flights … So we went to Rome for three or four days … I mean family is very important to me, and the year before it was my dad's 70th birthday so we went to Prague with him and we kind of felt we really had to do something for my mum as well for her 60th … my sister, who didn't come, did contribute towards the price of the flights and things like that. (No. 3, male architect, early thirties)

One woman explains how she and her partner invited her parents to Las Vegas to see the singer Celine Dion on their 35th wedding anniversary:

> My mum and dad are big fans of Celine Dion … It was actually their 35th wedding anniversary and it was kind of a Christmas present, anniversary present and birthday present all rolled into one – just a very nice treat. Even when we went to see Celine Dion we got superb tickets. We were five rows from the front and we could see everything. And she could see us and we could see her and it was just amazing. (No. 18, female personal trainer, early thirties)

These offspring show their love for their parents by giving them a special holiday. The obligatory nature of the holiday to Rome is shown by the fact that it takes place despite a lack of money and the need for the absent sister's financial contribution. These gifts are more than tickets to see Rome, Celine Dion and Las Vegas; they represent a desire to be with the parents and have quality time, for experiencing the places and events *together* as a family. The concert in Las Vegas does not only offer proximity to a famous star, but also to each of the family members; it evaporates the 40 or more miles (they live in Liverpool and Chester respectively) that separate their homes and prevent them from having as much co-presence at home as they would otherwise like.

So the interviews also bring out the significance of tourist travel as a way of being intimate with one's close family. As we discussed in Chapter 3, tourists are not only encountering other bodies and places but also travel with significant others.

This following quotation illustrates how an extended family that all live close to each other nonetheless embark on tourist travel to bring the family 'a little closer together' after it suffered from 'a couple of deaths':

> The second time it was like a big family holiday. There was like 19 of us who went. So it was kind of organized for everybody really … We'd had a couple of deaths in the family and it was in quite a short space of time, within a couple of weeks of each other. It kind of brought the family a little bit closer together. So everybody decided right let's all … we've not had a holiday together before so let's all go away now. (No. 24, male sales adviser, mid-twenties)

Visiting and Hosting

VFR tourism is distinct in that it requires more than just economic capital. It also needs distant friends or family members to offer hospitality. Distant connections enable people with modest incomes to travel further than their income would otherwise allow. The male porter, mapped in the previous chapter, has a 'rich' uncle in San Francisco:

> I have been to San Francisco twice [within the last couple of years] … he [uncle] said 'oh you must come' … The company that my uncle was working for, he got all these air miles … I stayed at my uncle's place … Yeah, he's always got things planned, like we'll go and watch a baseball or basketball game. He's always got tickets there waiting for us, so it's quite cheap when we get there. (No. 21, male university porter, mid-twenties)

Here we again see how business travel and leisure travel overlap, since business travel generates air miles that generate leisure travel for others. This is one example of how VFR tourism involves touristic places and events and *yet* is network strengthening at the same time. Some respondents describe how they go abroad more often now that their parents have bought a villa in Spain or France:

> Well we've just bought a house so we are planning on not putting all our money into that [tourist travel] this year. However, we will go to Majorca because it's a family home so it just costs us the flights. So yeah we will do that. (No. 14, sales manager, mid-twenties)

The lure of free accommodation means that people living in what are deemed to be interesting places are especially likely to receive visitors (in part against their will):

> I'm organizing a trip to Mexico because I know he's [friend] only there for another year, so there's no point on missing out on free accommodation … You know, say it was somewhere like Azerbaijan, I don't think I would be that keen on going, but you know Mexico, I'd quite like to go there. (No. 5, male architect, late twenties)

Another states:

I'm going there because I want to go back to Africa and it's a good excuse. If I know someone there already, he can like show us around and show us where the good spots are, where the dodgy spots are ... Yeah, more to see Africa, but yeah we will see him too. (No. 12, receptionist, early twenties)

This illustrates how free hospitality might be exploited to achieve cheap holidays rather than co-presence. This also means that VFR tourism might actually on occasions be 'damaging' to social relationships because it primarily takes place because of the place and the free accommodation, and not because of the relationship. Obligations of hosting might thus be a rather testing experience.

We have seen how much travel thus involves a specific combination of places *and* significant people; most tourists take a trip with significant others and they might visit or meet up with friends or kin. The respondents travel with their partner to visit parents in their hometown or their migrated parents in Spain or their best friend now living in Felixstowe or an old university friend now working in Berlin or head for a stag night in Amsterdam with a group of friends. So when they travel to friends or kin they simultaneously travel to particular places, and these places will be especially experienced through their friends and family members' accumulated knowledge of the place's attractions. These respondents' travel patterns illustrate how sociality matters in sightseeing and places matter in the visiting of other significant people.

Distant Connections and Travel

In Chapter 3 we discussed how new research spells out the significance of tourist travel for migrants and members of diasporic cultures. International tourist travel to see friends and relatives is particularly significant for the three migrants in this sample that were shown in the last chapter to possess stretched out networks.

The Irish male architect (No. 5) returned to Ireland three times in 2004. On each occasion it was coordinated as a self-directed package holiday where he toured various places to see friends, family members and the national rugby team playing crucial games, thus combining obligations to significant people and live events. So timing was crucial on these trips.

For the doorman (No. 24) and his family, mapped in the previous chapter (see Map 3), who lived 25 years in South Africa before returning to the UK, annual holidays to South Africa are essential even though they are expensive and prevent him from touring mainland Europe. It is very important to return home to stay in contact with, and introduce their daughter to their family as well as to the landscapes of South Africa. These visits also enable him to reunite with friends living in Cape Town, elsewhere in UK and Europe, as his transnational circle of friends and their families coordinate their holidays so that they visit Cape Town at the same time. He also explains how the last time that his family-in-law came to UK was straight after they had their first baby. They stayed for three months to help out with the baby and to provide general support.

Obligations and caring were also part of the reason why the female architect from Russia (No. 2) travelled to Russia three times in 2004:

> I was there in December and at New Year, then I was there ... at the beginning of summer to my best friend's wedding and then my granddad passed away so I went only three weeks after that ... My mum phoned me in the evening, I was in the office. I stayed in the office overnight just to finish off things, and booked flights first thing in the morning, called a taxi, called for passport and I was in Russia in about ... I don't know, less than a day after she phoned. He lived with us for 17 years. I really had to be there. I went for a week and then I went in December again – for Christmas. (No. 2, female architect, early thirties)

This illustrates how intimate networks of care, support and affection can be traced over geographical distance, as scholars of kinship and immigration have long known (see Chapter 2). This female architect speaks with her mother in Russia every Saturday morning for an hour or so and she is in more or less daily email contact with her brother living in Russia that needs her help with various issues. While caring at-a-distance works in most cases, the death of her granddad means that 'she really has to be there', to be in proximity with the rest of family. She has to care in a much more embodied and social way than is possible by just phone calls and emails.

Timing is everything; this woman has to be on time for the funeral and she is therefore in an acute rush to fulfil her work obligations and arrange the journey. This illustrates how the flexible and efficient coordination and travel depend upon access to, and skilful use of, phone, mobile, the internet, email, web pages as well as the financial means to buy last-minute tickets and to take taxis. This shows the independent importance of network capital.

Another example of how obligations to significant others, caring and complex family biographies can generate tourist travel relates to the UK-born porter (No. 19) with Indian parents and a husband born and bred in an Indian village. This couple and their four children can only afford[1] to travel to his family in India once every five years or so. They once went because her father-in-law was seriously ill and he had never seen his oldest grandchild: being very ill the grandfather was very eager to see his grandchild and they were eager to support their parents and be there in case

---

1 As she says:

> If it was just me and my husband ... it might not be too bad, but because it's like me and my husband and the five children and his mum ... Well I tried to calculate just for the summer ... just flight only was going to be over £5,000, that's without ... Because obviously when we go there we do have like family even still, we can't expect them to pay for us. Like my husband always makes sure that with the food and everything coming into the house, he was giving his sister the money, and she would buy the food. We've never relied, depended on them, because they don't have that much money themselves. So my last journey, when I went with three children and my husband and his mother, ... in a matter of like six weeks, we spent about £13–£14,000.

he passed away. The grandfather eventually recovered and is now living with them in England:

> Well my eldest daughter was four, and my husband's parents had never seen my children and they'd not seen their grandchildren basically. So I think because my father-in-law had become ill, he was ill and he wanted to see his son and wanted to see my children because they'd never seen them … at that point it was important for him to be there because his father was ill and he wanted to go and he wanted the children to see his parents. So I suppose because the parents are here now it's not been as important as it was at the time. (No. 19, female porter, late thirties)

Now that her husband's parents are living with them in the same house in the UK it is less important for them to visit India.

Catching Up

Trips abroad to catch up with busy friends living in the UK are also common (see Shove 2002). Long work hours, commitments to partners and dispersed social networks make it difficult for friends to meet up spontaneously at the same time, so meetings are coordinated in advance and tourist travel often brings networks together:

> My friends from back home in Chester, everyone does their own thing. It's quite difficult to all meet up at the same time. We've all got like our partners and things like that, and our partners aren't really from the same area so they don't really know each other very well. Quite often, if we are going to meet up, we try and go away or something together. (No. 11, male sales adviser, late twenties)

This is how another sales adviser explains a recent extended weekend trip to Amsterdam:

> It was more of a touristy holiday, a relaxing holiday. I went with four other friends as well. People I hadn't seen for a while. It was a catching up holiday. They mainly came from London. It was people that I hadn't seen whilst I was away in Barcelona. I had come back but they were living in opposite sides of London so it was still far enough. And then we decided to get together and go for a holiday. (No. 10, male sales adviser, late twenties)

The male architect, mapped in the previous chapter (see Map 4), possessing many distant connections explains how a recent stag night to Prague might turn out to be an annual event:

> … basically it was a circle of friends who I've known since I was at sixth form, college and university … It's very very rare that we're all in the same spot at any one time, all of us together, so there's been a lot of talk about arranging it as a yearly thing because it is so rare that everyone can meet up for personal reasons, some have got family, married or live far away or, you know, work commitments. It seems like a really good excuse just to

sort of say this year we're going to Berlin for three or four days ... (No. 4, male architect, early thirties)

He also talks about how he goes snowboarding once or twice a year and how these trips are important social events where people catch up with old friends, friends of friends and meet new people as new faces constantly join this revolving snowboard network stretching across the UK and Europe. On the last trip to Canada 'there were 12 of us ... people in Glasgow and Aberdeen ... people in London ... right down to people in East Grinstead and Surrey and stuff like that. I'm sort of in the middle.'

Weddings, Stag/Hen Nights and Cheap Airlines

A problem I have ... I find a lot of my holidays have been taken up with going to weddings and going to stag dos. This year I've got seven weddings to go to ... I'm going to have to take out a mortgage. (No. 5, male architect, late twenties)

Fulfilling these obligations through tourist travel will often be costly. This also means that mobile social networks may in effect exclude those who would otherwise meet up if less expensive travel was possible. In the quotation above we see how a male architect expresses his financial concern over the many weddings and stag nights he has to attend. Reflecting that the average age of the interviewees is 28.5, weddings, stag nights, hen nights and honeymoons trigger much tourist travel, especially among architects. Stag nights in vibrant places like Berlin, Amsterdam and Prague are now common given how low-cost airlines can assemble dispersed social networks in such places at little more cost than meeting up in the UK. As two respondents reflect:

It's [the stag night] in Berlin because the flights are cheap. It's a city where not everyone ... has been to ... if you look at it, it's cheaper than going to London for a stag do in terms of travel costs, which is excellent, to go to a foreign country cheaper than you can within your country. (No. 5, male architect, mid-twenties)

Well it's more interesting, isn't it? You can spend £60 going to Amsterdam and people are a lot more attracted to doing that than say meeting in Birmingham. And yet because it is so cheap there are a hell of a lot more places. (No. 4, male architect, early thirties)

Within recent years, budget airlines have compressed Europe's cities into a transnational network of cheap and accessible playgrounds:

Yes, definitely I wouldn't be able to do it if it was more expensive because Liverpool Airport is only 10 minutes from this office and I can often work a half-day and fly at lunch time or I can fly immediately after work. And I can be in Spain and I can be in Germany in less time than I would be in London. (No. 8, male architect, mid-twenties)

Many of our sample regularly embark on (extended) weekend trips with budget airlines to places such as Dublin, Barcelona, Berlin, Paris and Rome, in order to enjoy quality time with partners, to catch up with friends or family members, and to 'misbehave' at hen nights or stag nights.

Most interviewees agree that it is more or less obligatory to attend stag nights and especially the weddings of important friends and family members, even if it requires substantial travel:

> With weddings, it's a big thing isn't it? You only get married once, so if it's a close friend you definitely feel obligated … I can't think of one invite we've turned down. We've probably been to about three or four and we've got about five or six over the next two years to go to. All over the place … you would just have to go wherever they are really. Like I say, if it's in France or Greece or whatever. (No. 7, male architect, late twenties)

Faraway weddings mobilize otherwise immobile people and bring together friends and family members that seldom meet up because distance separates them. In the last chapter we discussed how a female personal trainer phones and emails her American friends weekly but hardly ever see them (see Map 2). Yet the next time they meet will be at her wedding, and she is touched that they will make her wedding, especially because one of them: '… has never been out of the United States. And to turn round and say I'm making the effort to your wedding, and she doesn't like flying either … and it's going to be nine, ten hours … I think to myself WOW' (No. 18, female personal trainer, mid-thirties). After the wedding, they will take these Americans on a guided tour to London to show their appreciation that they made the journey, as her fiancé – a fitness manager – explains:

> … we're very fortunate in the fact that none of the people that we know have ever been to the UK so they're desperate to come over anyway, and we've actually arranged it so that they will arrive a couple of days before the wedding, and we've also got a few days after the wedding before we go on our honeymoon so we can take these guys … almost like a group excursion to London … They are coming over here for our wedding to help us celebrate but they will also do their sightseeing as well. (No. 16, fitness manager, mid-thirties)

The obligatory nature of weddings creates dilemmas if they clash with other obligations, especially if others do not acknowledge them. As one dedicated Liverpool football fan reflects:

> I have a record of not missing a match for about ten years at home … this year my partner's cousin is getting married in April [on a Saturday] and [perhaps] it clashes with a home match … her auntie has invited everyone round to her house for a get together the day after the wedding … I'm not going to miss the wedding, I can't miss the wedding … but if Liverpool are playing on Sunday then I will be tempted to come up on my own to watch the match because I don't feel it's quite as important, but again that will really be frowned upon, so…. (No. 3, male architect, early thirties)

Not fulfilling social obligations can have significant social consequences; in this example, this architect will 'be really frowned upon' if he fulfils his obligations to his football friends rather than the guests at the wedding.

Obligations are thus not fixed in time and space, but are negotiated, contested and enforced. 'Moral work' is often required to remind people of their obligations. As one person says about the surprisingly big turn out for his wedding in Spain: 'I think my father probably put a lot of pressure on his brothers and sisters, my aunties and uncles, to come over from Ireland, because they were all there' (No. 6, male architect, early thirties). Perhaps this pressure was needed because no family members have connections with Spain. The couple got married in Spain because they wanted it to be special, and this was possible because they have wealthy friends that have retired to a well-known tourist spot that is connected to UK by budget airlines:

> So I was talking to a couple of friends of ours who … they're retirement age, 65, quite wealthy and they'd just bought a house over in Spain, a villa, a holiday home. And I was telling them my predicament. I said we just don't know what to do … We just want to go and get married somewhere. So they said why don't you get married near the villa in Spain? (No. 6, male architect, early thirties)

During the wedding preparations the architect and his fiancée travelled four times to Spain where they also enjoyed the hospitality of friends. This again illustrates how connections at-a-distance can afford possibilities for mobile lifestyles.

Weekend Touring and Significant Others

Most of the reported long-distance leisure journeys within the UK (more than 160 km) are (extended) weekend tours, and therefore involve at least one overnight stay (so qualify as tourist travel). Exceptions are one-day trips to football matches, mountain bike races in the countryside and so on. In Chapter 3 we discussed how most long-distance travel is tied up with visiting significant others, and most of the long-distance travel of these youngish peoples is to visit friends, kin and attend significant events; it is travel for social purposes. Relatively few of the journeys are simply excursions or holidays to particular sights within the UK.

Compared with one-day trips, tourist travel allows people to spend sustained, slow moving quality time together. When staying overnight there is no rush to catch the last train or worry about drinking too much to drive (the significance of meeting up in pubs and going for dinners are accentuated in many of the interviews!) or to catch up in a hurry. Rather than just having a meal for a few hours, they spend, say, 48 hours together.

Many of these meetings with friends and family take place at (extended) weekends. One respondent explained how: 'Normally about three nights. We don't normally go down for two nights. 'Longer than three nights you start getting in each other's way' (No. 24, male doorman, mid-thirties). Such tourist travel is relatively short because it takes place in private homes (with perhaps too little space for extra people) and through non-commercialized hospitality; it requires substantial domestic work and the guiding of visitors to interesting local places.

As hypothesized in Chapter 1, people compensate for the intermittence of meetings and the cost of transport (time, money and weariness) by spending a whole day or weekend or week(s) together, often staying in each other's homes. In other words, frequent yet short visits turn into intermittent yet longer periods of face-to-face co-presence, of hosting and visiting. Their meetings are less frequent but more intense and multifaceted: 'I often think that the people that are not local I only see two or three times a year, I have a stronger friendship with than the people I see every two or three weeks because it's quality time' (No. 24, male doorman, mid-thirties).

The last chapter documented that most people have a mix of close and distant connections. Their distant connections are typically very good friends known for a long time; they are deep-rooted friends that people are ready to travel for. The much-travelled architect mapped in Chapter 6 (see Map 4 above) says:

> I've got a lot of good friends in this office for example who I am establishing good relationships with, but you know you also have your best friends, don't you, the people you have grown up with over the years, there is quite a strong bond and you are prepared to make the effort to sort of go out and see them. And it's always rewarded – you are never disappointed. You know maybe I'll go to London and see some friends there and I know I'll have a really good time, and I'll come back and say I'm glad I went. It's better than sitting round the house all day and … it actually only costs you like £20 on the train if you buy it in advance. It's absolutely no effort at all for a much better quality of life sometimes …. (No. 4, male architect, early thirties)

Best friendships can thus cope with distance, because they have stood the test of time (see Chapter 6).

By comparison, friendships that are close by are often more fickle and less likely to endure if distance intervenes: ˙

> One have I lost contact with? A guy that I worked with on the cruise ship. Cracking bloke, he came onto the ship about three or four weeks after me, five years younger, got on like a house on fire, really good bloke. With us both working in the same industry, big into fitness, we would work out all the time. We actually had a week when we were in dry dock so the ship was shut down for a week. So we had two weeks rather. So we spent a week in Miami, went up to Florida, did all that. We were close. When I finished my contract he was about another two months behind me. He lived in Ipswich, and we would speak on the phone quite regularly, saying 'oh we're going to have to meet up', 'we're going to have to meet up', and yet we never did. And then gradually it turned from telephone calls to emails, and from emails it was like 'oh I got married last week'. And it was like ah, right, OK. (No. 16, male fitness instructor manager, mid-thirties)

Guilt Trips

Why do people travel? Tourist-type travel to see friends and relatives is particularly widespread in our sample amongst those who went to university. One Liverpool-based architect, who grew up in Warwick and went to university in Plymouth and Liverpool, reflects upon why he spends many hours on the road every second week:

> I think it's because I now live in Liverpool and my family and my school friends are still back in Warwick, and I went to university in Plymouth so I've got friends from Plymouth, and then I've got friends in London ... Some people I know in London were school friends, some people were at university in Liverpool, some people were at university in Plymouth, and they've gone to London. (No. 8, male architect, mid-twenties)

This explanation is in fact incomplete, as many journeys also result from his partner's equally stretched out social network. As he says: 'Well, last weekend I drove down to High Wycombe near London. My wife's grandmother is ill, we think she will die soon so we went to visit her'.

Indeed the interviews reveal how tourist travel is rarely an isolated decision pursued by individual agents but a collective action involving friends, family members, partners and their friends and family members. When these people talk about where they travel and why, they make references to complex relationships with (two sets of) family and friends. Their travel accounts are highly relational, just as their residential accounts (as shown in the previous chapter). People are entangled in social dramas wherein travel depends upon negotiation, approval and guilt, and have individual/social consequences. When we also take into account that many family events are more or less obligatory then we begin to explain how tourist travel has little to do with simple personal choice. In many instances 'guilt trips' set in motion physical trips:

> ... I don't like going [to the family in Italy] I must admit. I'm not a massive fan of going. But I did ... my mum wanted me to go ... Yeah, because I get the old guilt trip and then I feel like I have to go. (No. 22, male doorman, early twenties)

Indeed if people are absent at a compulsory family get together, it will be noted and their social face is likely to be damaged:

> ... [my partner's] family are very rigid in the fact that there are certain days of the year like Easter, Boxing Day where it's a kind of compulsory family get together, so you have to make that effort to go down there. Your absence would be noted if you weren't there. (No. 3, male architect, early thirties)

For many people, being in a relationship means travelling a lot: they are likely to have two sets of parents, brothers and sisters, uncles and aunts, grandparents as well as friends. This indicates that we cannot understand long-distance travel patterns if the individual is taken as the unit of analysis (which is the case in most transport research). Individuals are enmeshed in networks that both enable and constraint possible individual actions. This also means that weekend touring can be especially stressful:

> ... we've got different groups of friends, her friends and my friends who live in London. And I actually hate going to London because we've got so many friends that are down there, so when you go down there you feel you have to try and see everyone, and at the end you come back on the Sunday and you wish you had another couple of days off. It just never feels like a weekend when you go down there. And there will always be arguments because someone will find out that you've been down to London but you purposely haven't told them because you know you can't fit them in. (No. 5, male architect, late-twenties)

This illustrates how such travel and visiting are effectively networking, at times enjoyable and stimulating, at times testing and demanding. Social life conducted at-a-distance and tourist travel is certainly not cost-free with regard to either money or time.

Movement and (In)flexibility

> ... I was discussing with my wife last week that it would be horrible not having a car because of the weekends. We don't use the car during the week very much. When it's local we cycle. Then at the weekends it's fantastic. It means it's achievable. (No. 8, male architect, mid-twenties)

Most national long-distance travel within Europe is car based (Hubert and Potier 2003). This is so amongst our interviewees because it is thought to be cheaper *and* more flexible. As a male architect says:

> I'm always [travelling] with my wife and if there's two people in a car it's always the cheapest I find. I think the train's very expensive. Probably the main reason is the convenience because you have your own timetable, you can go when you want to, you can come back and you can go exactly where you need to be. And often we use the car when we get to the destination. (No. 8, male architect, mid-twenties)

Another makes a similar argument:

> We try to use the car if possible, it's much more flexible and cheaper, I guess. When we go and visit parents it is always pretty much by car. It is rare that we use the train for that. I use the train for work but I find that pretty good value. ... [My partner's] dad and my parents live in rural areas and once you get there you need to have that access to a car to get around. You couldn't drive down to where my mum and dad live and get a train anywhere. You'd have to get the train to Shrewsbury, which is the main town, and they would have to come and pick you up from the station, it's about six miles away. And the rest of the weekend you'd spend asking for lifts or whatever. (No. 3, male architect, early thirties)

So long-distance travel by car is cheaper than by train because these people undertake such journeys with friends or partners (unlike in the USA where Putnam (2000) reports that people drive alone on 70 per cent of car journeys). They can share the cost of the petrol while there is no rebate when travelling together by train. In this sense cars are economically flexible. This also explains why respondents in relationships especially found long-distance travel by train 'very expensive'. While most people find commuting by train 'pretty good value', this is not so with long-distance travel undertaken with others.

These respondents also praise the car for affording temporal and spatial flexibility with regard to the route and time schedule. Cars avoid much of the timetabling involved in most public transport. It is possible to leave late by car, to miss connections and not least to travel in a relatively timeless fashion (see Urry 2004c). This is desirable since weekend trips often involve visiting people in more than one place. The flexibility of cars and inflexibility of trains are very pertinent in remote or rural areas where public transport often is insufficient. Some argue that their social life would suffer dramatically without a car because public transport is time consuming and draining. The female personal trainer (see Map 2) from the suburbs of Manchester with parents in the Wirral explains the 'pains' she would have to endure if travelling there by public transport:

> Well, yes. I would have to get from the house on the bus, then to Manchester, then from Manchester to Liverpool. Then I'd have to get another train over from Liverpool to the Wirral. Then there'd have to be another bus. It would take me at least two hours if not more. So the car is just so convenient. I don't know what I'd do without a car … I would see them less, if I didn't have one. (No. 18, personal trainer, mid-thirties)

Without the car she would meet her family less often. Here the car is an indispensable part of their network capital. The social fabric of this family would suffer without extensive car use (and this presents a major challenge to those providing public transport).

For most of these youngish people without children, cars are not essential for their weekly life. However, it is 'horrible not having a car because of the weekends', because it is difficult to meet regularly with distant others if relying upon public transport. Most respondents regard trains as expensive, unreliable (especially at weekends because of engineering work) and rigid with regard to route and time schedule. However, sometimes trains can appear flexible and cars inflexible. A few respondents praise trains for their material affordances in relation to long-distance travel, such as relaxing, sleeping and reading (see also Lyons and Urry 2005). An architect who normally drives to work explains why he travels to London by train:

> [I like trains] because I read. I take lots of things to keep my mind occupied. … it is a lot more satisfying than driving, easily. I mean you can arrive there with your head spinning from too much driving, dehydrated, needing the toilet. (No. 4, male architect, early thirties)

Compared with train journeys where one can sleep, read, talk, eat, text, write, drink or relax after a good dinner or pub visit, cars seem constraining and demanding (not least for the driver). Indeed one architect who applauds cars later expresses ambivalence:

> I find the drive down to London quite … in some ways I am kind of contradicting what I said, but the trip down to London is a bit of a bind. It is a four-hour car journey and the petrol costs are actually quite high for that. If … [tickets] were a lot cheaper, I think we definitely would get the train down there more often. (No. 3, male architect, early thirties)

And when asked whether he prefers train or car journeys, he replies:

> I actually quite like train trips. I quite enjoy … it is much more relaxing to get a book, to be able to read, to listen to music if you want to do that, but it is just a lot more comfortable I think than driving a lot of the time, although you do have if you're driving the flexibility of being able to stop if you want to. (No. 3, male architect, late twenties)

It is thus wrong to see cars as inherently flexible and public transport as inherently inflexible. The respondents that commute to work by train partly do so because it allows them to relax, read newspapers, listen to music on their MP3 player, text message and carry out light office work, such as updating the personal diary, reading documents and journals. In major cities such Manchester and Liverpool with extensive public transport, congestion and few parking spaces, buses and especially trains are often more flexible for commuting to work. There is nothing that we may call flexible about a car caught up in 'morning queues and parking problems' (Hagman 2006). But for city-dwellers cars are flexible when touring rural areas, visiting smaller towns and travelling between multiple places within a short period of time, such as over a weekend.

Tourist Travel and Migration

In Chapter 3 we discussed how tourist travel and migration are complexly folded into each other. Around one-third of respondents express the desire to migrate, often to 'hotter climates'. These desires are largely the result of tourist travel. They yearn to live in Southern France, Southern Spain, Thailand, Australia and Canada; these are places they fell in love with through (repeated) tourist visits. One respondent elucidates how he and his partner regularly travel to his parents-in-law's second home in Spain where he feels 'at home' and plans to live there in the near future because of its apparently laidback culture and many hours of sun and the sea (No. 11). Another explains how he goes on holidays abroad in order to become a qualified diving instructor so that eventually he can set up a diving business in Canada or Thailand (No. 15).

None of those planning to migrate express the fear that they will lose contact with friends and family. They believe that migration these days is easy because cheap flights, text messages and email have made the world 'smaller'. Thus migration no longer implies lost connections:

> In today's day and age and society, it would be a lot easier to emigrate than it would have been, say, 30 years ago, because if you did that 30 years ago … it's very hard to communicate, it's very hard to travel and see people. I think you'd be quite isolated if you did that, whereas like you say through today's technology and things, you are a phone call away, a text away, planes flying almost every … all around the world now. (No. 15, male fitness instructor manager, mid-thirties)

This respondent wishes to migrate to Thailand or preferably Canada because his family have 'seen and heard how nice it is. So I know that if I settled there, they would come over …. So, yeah, definitely the location has to be somewhere feasible for people to come out and see', that is, to keep the networks alive (No. 15, male fitness instructor manager, mid-thirties).

Conclusion

This chapter has examined why respondents travel. We began with documenting the significance of long-distance leisure travel, showing that on average the respondents make almost one longer UK journey each month and more than two journeys abroad each year. While leisure travel is still concerned with traditional tourism, it seems that more travel is concerned with networking and meeting up. At least a third of their journeys abroad and the vast majority of UK journeys are predominantly about co-present meetings with significant others.

While communicative travel is crucial to dispersed social networks, its substitution effect upon corporeal tourist travel is small so far, because it connects dispersed networks in spaces of enjoyed co-presence. This makes travel essential for many:

> [Travel] is essential. I don't think we could go on just by making emails and phone calls. It is very necessary for us to go and see friends and family … I think it would be emotionally bad for us if we didn't. We need to travel. (No. 10, sales adviser, late-twenties)

Throughout the chapter we have shown how leisure and tourist travel are not isolated exotic islands but significant sets of social and material relations connecting and reconnecting disconnected people in face-to-face proximities where obligations and pleasures go together. Long-distance travel is necessary to fulfil social obligations, such as attending weddings, stag nights, hen nights, birthdays, Christmas parties, funerals, reunions, visiting and having quality time with significant others. To be able to travel is thus crucial for social capital, for the ability to sustain intimate bonds with, and meet obligations to, close yet faraway people. So *contra* Putnam discussed in Chapter 2, we have shown how travel can produce social capital in societies with dispersed social networks.

Transport policies thus have crucial implications for the production of social capital. Unreliable, slow and expensive transport has detrimental effects upon a given society's social capital. When asked what consequences higher prices for petrol and train tickets will have for their essential travel, the same person provides an ambivalent answer:

> I think it would reduce [our visits to our family] because of the costs. I would have to limit the amount of times I would go and see them. But, saying that, it costs me quite a lot to go over to Ireland, buying two plane tickets to go and see my girlfriend's family. So even though it's quite expensive to go and see her family, it would be the same essential scenario. So we'd still make the time and spend the money to do it because it's something you have to do ... you feel obliged to go and see the family. So definitely the obligation is there to go and see my family regardless of price, regardless of time. (No. 10, male sales adviser, mid-twenties)

This quote highlights how people are forced to undertake necessary and obligatory travel even with high costs. Travel is for many people a necessary evil. By contrast with sightseeing- or sunbathing-type tourism, necessary and obligatory travel appears less determined by price as it cannot be disregarded or substituted without significant consequences. Even with higher prices and poorer services, most people will still undertake what they see as necessary travel.

Whereas the concept of sightseeing used to be a fitting basis for leisure and travel theory, networking now seems as pertinent. There are a number of key elements about this networking approach to thinking through the nature of tourism. First, networking highlights how tourist travel is a social practice that involves embodied work, of scheduling, travelling, visiting, guiding, hosting, cleaning and so on. In other words net*working* is in part work.

Second, travel patterns are relational and embedded within social networks and their obligations; they are not free floating and unrelated to everyday patterns of social life, of family and friendship. Tourists are increasingly to be found in everyday places and have actually for once literally gone off the beaten track.

Third, tourist travel involves 'network capital' and the generation of 'social capital' through facilitating richer and more interdependent patterns of sociability.

Fourth, tourist travellers should be seen as producers of social relations as much as they are passive consumers.

Finally, places will be very variably experienced through being visited through these different modalities, as a place of sightseeing, a place of re-meeting friends, a place of family encounters, a place for professional/business meetings, a place of meeting at specific events and so on. What thus is important is deciphering the interconnections between places, events and sociabilities.

Chapter 8

Coordinating Networks and Travel

Introduction

The last chapter showed that much travel stems from various compulsions to proximity, the desire and need to be corporeally co-present with significant others often living elsewhere. This chapter now examines contemporary coordination systems that enable such intermittent meetings. We have argued that little research has paid attention to networking practices of coordinating networks and travel. Elaborating upon Chapters 3 and 4, this chapter examines how corporeal travel and communicative travel fold into each other, and how email and mobile phones enhance corporeal travel. We show that one reason that corporeal and communicative travel both increase is that communications are intricately tied up with coordinating such travel. How respondents organize their travel and co-presence with network members through the internet, emails, and mobile calls and texting is examined in this chapter. First, we show how the respondents routinely mediate communicative co-presence on the move. Second, we explore how network meetings are coordinated and depend upon the possession of network capital. Third, by comparison with pocket watches and landline phones, we show that mobile phones and email under specific circumstances afford fluid and flexible meeting cultures less dictated by fixed appointments and clock-time. This indicates how clock-time and punctuality are supplemented by what we term *flexible network time*.

Mobile Phones and Communications on the Move

In Chapter 3 we discussed research showing how widespread mobile phone ownership affords small worlds of communicative co-presence in the midst of absence, distance and disconnection. Absent others are a call or text message away so people can be in communicative propinquity with significant others even in a sea of strangers (Roos 2001; Molz 2004). Nowhere do people seem more busy calling and texting than when in motion or transit, and modern cities are thus no longer characterized by isolation but by connectivity, by private worlds of perpetual talk at-a-distance. Mobile phones are described by Ito, Okabe and Matsuda as 'personal, portable, pedestrian' (2005). Trains, buses, cars, streets and waiting lounges are now sites for much communicative co-presence, as travel time can be made productive (Lyons and Urry 2005).

The interviews reveal how respondents routinely conduct mediated communicative co-presence while on their lonely route to the supermarket, to home from work and while on longer journeys:

> I will sometimes walk into work if the weather is not great, or if I walk up to Sainsburys which is a mile away from the house, I will always take my phone and I will always phone somebody while I'm on that walk just to have a chat and so it's not such a boring way. (No. 11, male sales adviser, late twenties)

People may be physically isolated in the city but they are communicatively connected to their networks, so on one level the city experience is less lonely (and insecure) compared with when Simmel wrote. A security doorman brings out how he and his mother transform lonely travel time into social time by calling each when commuting to and from work. As a result, they have more or less daily exchanges despite living far from each other and working different hours:

> On my way to work I'll always ring my mum. For me it's a 10-minute walk to work so I think I can ring them and have a chat to them for 10 minutes, so I'll normally do that ... whereas my mum, when she's driving home on a long-distance business trip, she'll always ring me then when she's in the car. She's got one of those ... you know the speaker things in cars, so she uses that ... obviously because she can keep on driving. (No. 22, male doorman, early twenties)

That cars are particular good places to talk is stressed in the following quotations:

> I make my phone calls more at weekends ... Maybe, for instance, I'm going to Preston, so I think right, I go down the diary and I'll just make my calls whilst my husband's driving ... people who I think I have not caught up with or not managed to get to, I will do it whilst we're on the journey so I'm not wasting time at home ... (No. 19, female porter, late thirties)

> I always speak on my headset now on the way home [from work]. I am always on the phone on my way home, always ... I just feel it makes use of the time really ... I do now and again text while I'm driving. (No. 14, male sales manager, mid-twenties)

Much research stresses how cars isolate people in private cocoons with no contact to the outside world. Yet now that mobile phones have become ubiquitous travel partners people are in a sense never alone and they coordinate many of their calls to take place precisely while they are on the move. Thus cars, buses and trains become places of much communicative travel and this connects them to the outside world, involving an always-on intimate connection (see Ito, Okabe and Matsuda 2005).

This can described as networked individualism. When networks are stretched out and overlap little there is less likelihood of quick, casual, unplanned meetings and fewer possibilities for walking in order to meet up (by Western standards). So people need to travel to maintain their networks and they thus rely upon cars or public transport, upon being out and about. In Chapter 7 we saw that respondents make some 10 longer UK journeys per year, primarily to visit significant others and attend obligatory events. Much time is thus spent communicating with people to *coordinate* such co-presence, and this necessitates what we call network capital.

Network capital involves access to communication channels. Each day the architects 'surf the web' for their professional work, and for news, cultural events, cheap flights, travel information, and so on. And they email, both professionally and socially, sending around eight private emails a day. By comparison, the two other occupations email less both professionally and socially; they receive some seven private emails weekly. Our research shows a correlation between the number of professional and private emails: people that email professionally also email much socially and vice versa. The architects are richer in such capital than the other two groups.

Nevertheless, all respondents in the sample own a mobile phone and so do all their friends and most family members. Most mobiles are turned on and at-hand for 24 hours a day; they are only switched off and silent at work and occasionally when socializing. The respondents disagree whether it is reasonable to use mobile phones when meeting socially but they note that many people do. When people turn their mobiles off they fear missing out:

> I suppose you're afraid … I think just having the phone turned on just makes you sort of know that you definitely won't miss out on anything. For all you know a friend could phone you at work and ask you if you want tickets for a football match that night or something, and obviously if you didn't have that phone with you, you'd be speaking to them the next day and they'd be saying I had tickets for last night. So it gives you opportunities that you maybe wouldn't have had before. (No. 11, male sales adviser, late twenties)

All respondents make calls and text messages with their mobile. The youngest in the sample use their mobiles most, but there are no major differences between the three subgroups. Mobile phones are crucial networking tools and are used as calendars, address books, telephone books and indeed watches (pocket watches are now often fashion gadgets). They produce and/or store music, games, photos, articles and messages, and these are circulated amongst network members, sometimes over great distances. Mobile phones are thus multitasking technologies much more complex than one-dimensional landline phones.

Mobiles have become 'travel partners' so that people feel incomplete if they set off without them: 'I'll know about it if it's not there because you know you can't leave the house and you think something's missing. It's got to be with me definitely. It's got to be with me' (No. 10, male sales adviser, late twenties). They describe their mobile phones as prosthetic, as physically coterminous with their bodies. They allow them to be proper social beings. Without mobiles, people are lost: 'I've lost it once. This sounds so bad, but it was the worst week of my life. I didn't have a clue what I was doing or anything … the worst thing was all my numbers were on it' (No. 22, male doorman, early twenties). More or less everyone expresses, not without a little shame, that their present life depends upon mobile phones because they are 'great social tools'. As an architect says:

> I hate to say it … I got my first mobile about [19]99 … [they used to be] extravagant, frivolous. But as soon as I got one I suddenly realized that I just couldn't live without it. It's been a great … yeah it's a hell of a social tool. (No. 4, male architect, early thirties)

Mobile phones are a necessary evil, a natural part of the human body that is always at-hand. So when people misplace their mobile they are disabled. They can no longer talk with absent others and they are disconnected from their networks. Mobile phones are network's 'lifelines' because young people now remember few numbers since mobiles store them. So a landline connection cannot substitute for a lost mobile phone. When such youngish people lose their mobiles they explain how they are in a sense lost with non-connectivity and are likely to have fewer face-to-face interactions as a result.

Coordination Tools

Chapters 6 and 7 examined how respondents use communications to simulate face-to-face co-presence. But the significance of mobile phones and email for the coordination of meetings and travel are striking findings from our research. This can particularly be seen with respect to email:

> Today there was an acknowledgment of the Travel Lodge booking that I did. Another one was we've had a tournament cancelled and obviously it was distributed to the team … another one I got today … I always get together with my girlfriends from school on a Thursday evening, so it was making arrangement … I don't chat, I don't gossip on email. It's all arranging. (No. 1, female architect, early thirties)

For this female architect, who coaches a youth sports team, the typical email involves coordination. Like most others she books holidays, flights and accommodation on the internet, because she finds it cheaper and less time consuming than making the trip to a travel agent. Every second week or so she undertakes a longer journey with her partner or with the team she coaches.[1] She also uses the internet to arrange

---

1   Virtually all interviewees occasionally use the internet to secure cheap air ticket with budget airlines such as Ryanair and Easyjet, and they all agree that the internet is much better value than going to a travel agent. Indeed, the internet is sometimes said to produce more tourist-type travel:

> Yeah, it's so much easier [with the internet], just at the flick of a button…. It was about a month ago when I was thinking I'll take Sharon away to Rome for our anniversary, and for two of us, two return flights and four nights in a hotel in Rome was £190, and you know … say 10 years ago you would never get anything like that. You wouldn't be able to just go on get a flight from there, get a hotel from over here, and see what happens when I get there. (No. 21, male porter, mid-twenties)

The popularity of the internet as 'market place' for travel and tourism means that many short-distance trips to the 'local' travel agent are saved. So people with easy access and knowledge of using the internet are often likely to travel cheaper than people who may well be poorer

matches and tournaments across the UK. And she coordinates her weekly meetings with local friends by email.

Distant connections often require coordination by email, especially if many people are involved and long-distance travel is necessary:

> You do find a lot of emails are for weekends that you organize … Yesterday I had an email because my wife and me are organizing a weekend to go away to the Cotswolds, so we are renting a cottage. There's six of us, eight of us going. So obviously there's a lot of emails coming in, being sent round, saying I can do such and such a weekend … . And then you get one back saying it's going to cost us, you know, £100 each for the weekend, can you send the money, post a cheque to me. (No. 5, male architect, late twenties)

Emails are time-effective since one message can be sent to multiple people and they can then reply to the whole network with additional information, without distorting or deleting the initial or succeeding emails. Dates and venues are thus remembered and accessible for recollection in mailboxes, preventing much additional coordination at a later stage. Everybody within this network thus shares and has equal access to the same information and we may therefore hypothesize that the task of organizing is more equally distributed. And paradoxically this seems to produce *more* meetings:

> It makes it easier to meet up with people because there is less effort involved in writing a small message and sending it out to a number of people in terms of coordination and getting people together. … For instance, when it was my stag do a couple of years ago; my best man did it all by email and it worked wonderfully well because you get this kind of coordination of dates when people are available, when they are not … So rather than that kind of confusion that occurs when you are going from one person to another and then going back … you have got this situation where everything is … transmitted to everybody from one source. (No. 3, male architect, early thirties)

Text messaging provides some of the same affordances:

> Well last week I organised 20 of us to go to a greyhound meeting. I didn't speak to one person; it was all done by text message. I didn't speak to one person … I just write a message, sent it all to everyone, I said if you want to come, send me a reply, I'll book you a ticket. Everyone replied, I booked a ticket and we all turned up and that was it. (No. 22, male doorman, early twenties)

This flexibility and ability of emails and text messages to travel contrasts with telephone calls that always involve one-to-one talk and do not produce an entry in an archive. Group coordination by phone conversation requires a central hub where all information passes through, so one person is in charge of synchronizing busy and fragmented diaries. This is a time-consuming and certainly not cost-free task, as each link often calls, or has to be called, more than once so as to achieve coordination.

---

who have to rely upon travel agents. However, apart from tickets for travel and holidays, the interviewees seldom substitute shopping trips with internet shopping.

Emails and text distribution lists have made it easier and cheaper for dispersed networks with highly desynchronized diaries to arrange and rearrange meetings.

Gibson's (1979) notion of affordances highlights how certain technologies enable/ produce some kinds of actions and not others. We discussed how text messages afford collective, non-centralized coordination that make group coordination smoother than with one-to-one communications. Yet it is sometimes neglected how affordances are context dependent, it matters where they are placed and how they are performed. Communication technologies afford possibilities but do not determine how people perform them. They are preformed and performed (Larsen 2005, 2006). This is also the case with coordination tools. As one respondent reflects: 'If you are walking, it is easy to phone. If you are on a train, it's warm and you don't have to wear gloves, then it's easy to text. It's just where you are at the moment of communicating' (No. 2, female architect, early thirties).

Place matters with email because it requires a computer and internet connection, and currently most respondents only have access to the internet at work or at home (except, of course, with wireless communications and place-independent blackberries). The architects coordinate much of their social life by email because they have access to personal work emails and work computers with internet connections. Much of the architects' private email communications takes place at work:

> I've got internet access at work ... I can use that any time. It's supposed to be for work but we all use it for other things as well. I've got internet at home but not broadband though ... because we have both got internet at work so we don't spend too much on it. (No. 7, male architect, late twenties)[2]

Many of their other friends, especially those from university, also have access to email at work: '... most of my friends from university have email at work, so while they are at work they will email me saying let's do something at the weekend' (No. 1, female architect, early thirties).

The rest of the respondents do not have such 'access' at work and they email less and as a result prefer mobile phones to coordinate their social life. Email for them is intermittently performed in order to communicate with significant others, predominantly at-a-distance (see Maps 1, 2 and 3 above).

---

2   However, emailing at work is primarily for quick coordination, gossip or jokes rather than the letter-kind of emails examined in Chapter 6. As one architect says when asked if she emails at work:

> Sometimes my brother writes ... he has been quite low recently, so sometimes he just comes on-line for a few moments ... where are you both? I say I am here, we're busy, just to find me sort of thing, talk to you later that sort of thing. I dunno, sometimes I get very long emails I just don't have time to read. In the evenings or weekends I write long letters to my friends. So I don't really use working time unless it's just a couple of lines. Oh one friend of mine she was asking me questions, I need to know it now, I want to invite my mother from Russia so what do I do? How much money do I need in my account? So I replied immediately. (No. 2, female architect, early thirties)

Despite working in open offices, architects email privately because emailing – unlike 'noisy' phoning – is 'covert' within networked computer landscapes. The much-travelled architect whose life was mapped in Chapter 6 says:

> You would be on the phone and people are watching the time you are spending talking … Whereas with email it is a lot more covert and I think people spend a lot more time on the email, even I do. You know, you are all supposed to be working but you're all communicating, and you can have a big social event if you like. … At the moment I'm trying to arrange a snowboarding holiday, and there's about five or six of us all over the country, and you can have a little chat during the day. It's almost like you're down the pub having a bit of a social chat over a beer. (No. 4, male architect, early thirties)

While at work he coordinates a large social event with dispersed friends while they are also at work. Here the distinction between coordination and meeting blurs as the coordination event produces communications to such an extent that 'it's almost like you're down the pub having a bit of a social chat over a beer'.

Architects also email colleagues and friends around the corner. Here the clandestine nature of email is also valued. One explains how he occasionally goes for secret lunches to gossip and discuss office politics with a few carefully selected colleagues. By coordinating the meetings by email they can better leave in silence. The architects' emails thus travel both short and long distances, while the other respondents' emails mainly travel lengthy distances (see also Chapter 6).

Email has largely substituted for phone calls when it comes to coordinating social life amongst these architects:

> It's taken over from the telephone definitely, because I don't take hardly any personal calls in work time, and it would have to be urgent to do that really … It's the speed at which you can do it, but also again the distribution lists. You don't have to phone four people up. The same information gets to all people at the same time. (No. 1, female architect, early thirties)

Here email distribution lists are praised for being flexible, time effective and almost instantaneous, as the same information gets to all people at the same time. However, email is only immediate if people are more or less continuously on-line and respond promptly to messages. Therefore, the architects continuously check their email accounts, so each time an arrival is announced they check the inbox to see whether it is something interesting: 'so there's this kind of intrigue about who it could be, when that little envelope pops up on the screen, it's like who is that, is it a friend, a joke or something, or is it work related' (No. 3, male architect, early thirties).

So, many smaller 'breaks' during the day are tied up with private emails, as good email conduct involves quick replies so as to make it as immediate as possible. Another aspect of this conduct is to employ a precise, fast and instrumental language and this distinguishes email from telephone conversations where a relatively lengthy exchange of pleasantries and personal news is expected. One architect explains why email is so effective at coordinating meetings:

> You don't have to talk round it. You can merely put in one line and you get an answer back in one line. There's no talking about how are you. There's no chitchat … whatever is in your head, you type and it's gone. By the time you're thinking what else you forgot to ask, and replies come back. That's the beauty of email. It is quick. Literally one line … 'What are you doing at the weekend?' If I picked up the phone, I can't just pick up the phone: 'What are you doing at the weekend?' I'm going to have to say: 'How are you and what have you been up to?' And you get into a full conversation. (No. 5, male architect, late twenties)

Partly along similar lines, another stresses that:

> … you write emails at the drop of a hat. Like you've got five minutes to spare. … 'Oh Chris has replied'. Oh I've got something to tell him and I'll just sit down and type it. You would never have spent five minutes 'Oh what shall I do, I'll write a letter'. Email is not time consuming. I don't have to go and put it into an envelope, buy a stamp, post it, you know … you send a letter and it might come back five days later with a reply. But with an email you can do a one-liner and then two minutes later even though they are in Egypt they reply. It is more like a conversation. (No. 4, male architect, early thirties)

While emails afford timeless travel through space, it is only when people make 'drop of a hat' or 'one line' messages rather than wordy letters and reply promptly that email is fast and resembles face-to-face conversations. The fast-paced, flexible nature of much email stems only partly from affordances but also from the specific cultures within different social groups of performance and writing.

Effective and fast group coordination by email thus requires that all network members email at work or at least check it daily. This is particularly the case with short-term planning. As this female receptionist from Manchester says:

> When I'm living in Devon with my parents, I don't tend to email my friends that are in the local area because I see them more often and I speak to them on the phone more often. So there's no need to email. By the time she's read her email, I'll have seen her three times. (No. 12, female receptionist, early twenties)

The architects also email much less in the evenings and weekends because at this time they are seldom on-line and they can speak freely on their phone, so they use mobile phones and especially text messages to reach each other quickly. Often people text message each other because calls can be disturbing for the receiver and a text message is richer and more precise in information than a recorded message in case the phone is put on silent mode.

People without access to email at work find email slow and inconvenient because it are not as ready at-hand as mobile phones are: '[I] use my mobile phone a million times more [than emails]. I just think it's easier, a lot easier, than logging on and … you've got your phone there, it's easier to use' (No. 14, sales manager, mid-twenties).

The doorman who recently organized a trip for 20 people to go to a greyhound meeting explains why he used text messages rather than email to arrange this evening:

> Because I don't know if they check it [email]. It's the instant factor of it that I like more than anything, the fact that they get it straight away. They don't have to go and check their emails and I don't have to go and check mine to get it back ... My phone ... beep[s], and I can sort of write down who's coming ... And that's why I use text messaging, because it's instant. And my phone is always with me. (No. 22, male doorman, early twenties)

Those respondents who are not architects only check their emails twice a week on average, which makes short-term coordination by email too slow and risky.

Texting can also afford secret gossip and coordination. Many young people have developed striking texting skills and with their mobiles 'on silent' they text inaudibly in unlikely places. This ensures that texting is instant:

> You can just sort of drop your hand under the desk and ... Well I don't have to look at mine, I can text without looking ... [for instance] ... I was sat in a lecture. My lecture was about to finish so I said meet me at one [o'clock] ... by the time I got there, he was there. (No. 22, male doorman, early twenties)

Fluid Coordination

This research also suggests that the strict punctuality that Simmel thought he observed in early modern cities and meeting cultures partly dissolves with 'liquid modernity' (Bauman 2000a; Geser 2004). The objective clock-time of pocket watches is supplemented with a more negotiated network time of mobile communications. Now people may bend clock-time, through texting that they are running late or by suggesting a new place or a later time to meet. While some respondents are annoyed that many have become 'sloppy' about being on time,[3] people seem able to get away with it if they inform those they are meeting that they are behind schedule. 'I think because everybody carries their mobile with them, it doesn't matter if you are late for something' (No. 16, fitness instructor manger, early thirties). Now it seems that there is less an obligation to be on time as to inform those friends or family members 'waiting' that one is, or just might be, late (this seems in contrast with much work life where people are expected to be on time and flexible punctuality is often also contested by older generations that still adhere to pre-fixed clock-time coordination). This is particularly evident on trains where every announcement of even a minor delay makes most passengers reach out for their mobile. All respondents feel obliged

---

3   As one respondent says:

Well I am a much-organized person and although I don't keep a diary, I don't miss appointments, but for a lot of my friends it is an opportunity for them to change their plans regularly. If they didn't have a mobile phone, then they would have to do what they organized. That's a personal hate of mine. (No. 8, male architect, mid-twenties)

to inform those waiting that they are late, so that they do not worry and perhaps can do something else in the meantime.

Whereas coordination was traditionally finalized with the departure for the meeting, it is now often negotiated and performed on the move, at least this is the case with youngish people. This contrasts with pre-mobile days when fixed appointments were the only choice (and these are still important for the more formal meetings we discussed earlier). One female architect reports how her group of friends often only make loose prior arrangements with regard to time; they use mobile phones to work out what we might call 'flexible punctuality':

> But flexible definitely because sometimes I won't arrange a time ... I mean obviously a vague like I'll meet you in there, but then I'd make a text as I get a taxi and say I'll be there in 10 minutes, whereas in the past you would have to phone earlier in the evening saying I would be there at 7 o'clock. (No. 1, female architect, early thirties)

And another says:

> Yeah. It's usually a loose arrangement, say meet up roughly 8 o'clock in this bar, but most of the time that changes. Because you've got mobiles, you can do that ... I'm running late or we've decided to go to a different bar, meet us in this bar or whatever. (No. 12, female receptionist, early twenties)

When these youngish people arrange to 'go out' they set a day (often by email) but they seldom arrange a specific time. Rather, they agree to 'speak' on that day to finalize the finer details and that email, call or text will be followed up by a last-minute call or text confirming that one is leaving the house or stuck in traffic or has found a better place to meet up. A male architect sums up:

> You arrange a day, it happened last week, myself and [partner] were going out with another couple so she asked me two days before what time we're meeting, and I said 'I don't know yet, we're just going out'. I'll speak to [friend] tomorrow, later. And then it can be three or four text messages or telephone calls before we know where we're meeting. (No. 6, male architect, late twenties)

This also means that much meeting coordination involves both email and mobile phones. This is especially so with long-distance travel. The initial coordination is often by email while mobile phones take over when the journey actually begins:

> It was a long weekend. We do it once a year ... all my friends from back home, we meet up in one place and we do poker nights ... The date was arranged by email but [not] the finer details ... when I was coming down, I'd be texting my brother and my friends to say can you pick me up from here. If he can't do it, I'll text the next one and so on ... I had to pretty much do it all when I was travelling on the train. So I spent five and a half hours going there, so all the time while I was on the train I was texting and talking. (No. 10, male sales adviser, late twenties)

To provide another example:

> When I got to London it was either text or calling to say: 'I'm about to reach London, where do I go?' and then once I reach London it's like: 'Right I'm in London, I'm at Archway, where the bloody hell are you?' type of thing. (No. 9, male architect, early twenties)

So in many cases there is a clear division of labour between email and mobile phones, a division tied up with their different affordances.

Yet sometimes mobile phones seem to rule out the need for preceding coordination:

> Saturday Liverpool played Manchester United. A whole group of us met up, I'd say probably about eight of us in the morning. And these people were all coming from different cities ... and we'd made no arrangements. I remember thinking that 'Oh, all I know is that they are coming to the match'. So the first sign I hear of anyone going to be in the city is a text message at about half-past 10 saying we're in Wetherspoons pub, where are you, because otherwise they could be in any pub, we don't have a regular place to meet. So I have a text from there, so I get the train into town, other people start getting the same kind of text messages, and before you know it, everyone's met at the same place. And so without the mobile you would really struggle ... So it's a lot more fluid. (No. 3, male architect, early thirties)

It would of course be a disaster to forget to bring the mobile or let it run out of battery power. Such flexible coordination is dependent upon systems and it would be impossible to be part of these flexible networks without a functioning mobile phone.

Sometimes coordination also occurs *during* meetings, when people have already met up in a café, bar or pub. Some respondents (especially the younger ones and singles) do not go out with one group but rather a larger mobile-phone-connected network of both strong and weak ties. They text each other about happening places, parties and interesting people, and they are therefore likely to meet with people that they did not begin the evening with:

> If I'm in one bar and they're in another, I might text them and say it's not very good here, really quiet or really busy, we'll come ... where are you and you'll go oh I'm in Varsity and it's really really good. So I'll go to Varsity then. It's just like having a constant network between all of you. (No. 22, male doorman, early twenties)

Another respondent says:

> If I'm out in the pub round here, there's a good chance that somebody will ring me up from another pub across town, and say 'Oh yeah we're having a drink' ... or somebody coming into town and wants to meet up with you. (No. 4, male architect, early thirties)

So going out in such fashion involves continuous coordination, negotiation and movement with people present as well as (temporally) absent others. This provides opportunities to meet new people and come across what are deemed to be happening places. Texting is often impromptu and informal, and one text will often be sent to several people. This also enables fluid meeting cultures with recurrent circulating invitations to join in:

> It might be like you're sitting in the office or five or six offices around Liverpool and say we're all going out for a drink, do you want to come. And it happens instantaneously sort of thing. It is more manageable because you've got that instant communication. (No. 4, male architect, early thirties)

With widespread mobile connectivity, there is no need to wait for people to return home before an arrangement can be made and remade. Our respondents explain how they often call friends to inform them that they are in the neighbourhood and enquire if they fancy meeting up for a quick beer or coffee:

> You can arrange more things spontaneously, whereas if you suddenly finish work and you fancy a pint, it is a lot easier to get hold of someone and say are you around, do you fancy a quick pint before you go home, whereas a few years ago it would have been a bit difficult. (No. 6, male architect, early thirties)

Such youngish people without family responsibilities have plenty of time for impulsive socializing with (weak) ties; informal mobile phone cultures ensure plenty of invitations at hand.

Informal Coordination and Weak Ties

We discussed in Chapter 3 research suggesting that interface-to-interface interaction prompt more 'courageous selves'. The impersonal, informal nature of group messages means that there is less chance of 'losing face' when flirting, contacting or inviting people out by text and email than by phone and especially in person, where there is no time to perform courteous rejections and mask blushing faces (Oksman and Turtiainen 2004, 326; see also Henderson and Gilding 2004). As one respondent says:

> Of course writing is a more flexible way of communicating because you don't have time to think when you are on the phone ... it is easy to control your reaction. You kind of take a deep breath. Gosh, I was nearly in tears on Friday and if it would be on the phone, oh pathetic. But my emails were quite sharp, very dry, there were no emotions there. (No. 2, female architect, early thirties)

One architect explains how he recently invited some new friends for dinner by email because it will be awkward if they have to 'perform' a quick unrehearsed decline while on the phone:

> I emailed out to some friends last week to come over for dinner next weekend, and because it is done by email, it's not quite so ... I don't want to put them in a position where ... oh I'm not sure, I'm not sure. It's easier to give them that time to think about it and come back with [an] answer. (No. 3, male architect, early thirties)

It was also stressed that it was easier to find and contact an old friend by email than by phone, because it is less intruding to email and less 'damaging to face' to be rejected by a non-replied email than by an awkward phone call. As one architect says:

> I haven't seen him since I left school, which was 10 years ago, because we've got a 10-year reunion this year. I was quite good friends with him, but never had his mobile phone number, never had his email address, and didn't know where he was. He's an actor and he's just come out in a blockbuster movie. And because of that I was able to track him down, his email address. Out of the blue I just felt I could write him an email just saying best of luck, delighted to hear ... I felt again email made it easy for me to just turn around and say look I know I haven't seen you in nine years, but delighted for you and I hope it goes really well for you and just ... email, hopefully talk to you soon. (No. 5, male architect, late twenties)

This research thus shows that people are bolder in whom they invite when they can hide behind the informal and/or collective nature of emails and especially text messages. In Chapter 2 we discussed how Granovetter (1983) showed the strength of weak ties for successful job searches. Mobile phones, with their multidestination messages, multiple contacts and informality, are perfect tools for distributing casual invitations to 'join in' and information about happening places to one's weak ties. The young student architect explains how he sends cinema invitations by text every week to a large network of people at the college where he lives, and people just text if they wish to 'join in' (this also precludes the potential awkward experience of having one-to-one phone conversations with one's weak ties). The significance of weak ties, informal co-presence and 'new faces' seem to increase dramatically in the era of text messages and email, as research reviewed in Chapter 2 suggests (see also Wittel 2001).

Conclusion

When social networks are stretched out and distant connections are common, it is difficult to meet up spontaneously. Meetings have to be coordinated spatially and temporally in advance. This chapter has demonstrated the changing nature of arrangements to meet. We have shown that there have been some striking changes in the methods of coordination – a shift from punctuality effected through clock-time to a negotiated fluid coordination effected through mobile communications such as email and especially mobile phone texts and calls. We have seen how the clock-time punctuality that Simmel argued coordinated early modern cities and meetings partly dissolves in 'liquid modernity', at least amongst youngish people (Bauman 2003). The clock-time of pocket/wrist watches is increasingly supplemented by a negotiated 'network' or fluid time of mobile communications. Now people can not only be on time or running early or late, but also 'refuse to accept' clock-time by emailing or especially texting that they are late or suggesting a new place or a later time.

This is further facilitated by the widespread shift from public transport to 'flexible car systems'. Whereas trains and pocket watches were early modern twins, mobile phones and cars are the late modern twins, both raging against past rhythms and timekeeping. This research suggests that the striking popularity of cars, email and mobile phones are tied up with how they bend modern timekeeping and afford a flexible, mobile social life, in an era where many networks are dispersed and coordination and travel are necessary for social life.

We also demonstrated how the greater spatial scale and personalization of networks make more important those 'coordination systems' that facilitate travel and make important meetings realized. The social sciences often neglect the technological systems that in part afford what sociologists like Giddens and Beck call 'individualization' (see Chapter 2). The chapter demonstrates that with greater 'individualization', there is paradoxically more dependence upon coordination systems. It is difficult to escape these systems of transport and communication since they coordinate social networks and sociability with others. The more individualized people might be, the more dependent they are on systems that connect them with others!

More generally, this chapter shows that travel and communications are complexly folded into each other. Transport *and* communication technologies are travel partners. This is a process of co-evolution, between new forms of social networking on the one hand, and extensive forms of physical travel, now often enhanced by new communications, on the other. These sets of processes reinforce and extend each other in ways that are highly difficult to reverse. This also means that crucial to the character of modern societies is network capital, comprising, most importantly, access to communication technologies, affordable and well-connected transport and safe meeting-places. Without sufficient network capital people will be socially excluded as social networks have become more dispersed.

In the final chapter we discuss some implications of this empirical research for future research and for policy.

Chapter 9

Research and Policy Futures

Travelling in a Shrunken World

This research has highlighted the centrality of corporeal travel to extended social networks. In particular the respondents take for granted the historically low costs of travel and communications and have developed social patterns that take advantage of new geographies of access. We have shown that while sightseeing used to be a fitting basis for thinking about why people travelled in their leisure time, networking is now at least as pertinent. Networking highlights how travel is a social practice that involves embodied work of scheduling, travelling, visiting, guiding, hosting, cleaning and so on (networking is effectively work); that travel patterns are relational and embedded within social networks and their complex obligations; that travel involves tools and resources; that there are marked variations in access to such network capital; and that tourist travel often develops and produces social capital.

In particular we showed the embodied making of networks, performances and practices of networking. Social networks come to life and are sustained through various practices of networking, of email, forwarding messages, texting, sharing gossip, performing meetings, making two-minutes of bumping-into-people conversations, attending conferences, chatting over a coffee, meeting up for a drink and spending many hours on trains or on the road or in the air to meet up with friends, family members, workmates and partners.

Physical travel is especially important in facilitating those co-present conversations, to the making of links and social connections, albeit unequal, that endure over time. Such connections derived from co-presence can generate relations of trust that enhance both social and economic inclusion. Most people's biographies and mobilities are to be seen as relational, connected and embedded rather than individualized. People are enmeshed in social networks wherein actions depend upon negotiation, approval and feelings, and these in turn have social and emotional consequences. Individuals are enmeshed in networks of pleasure, obligation and duty that enable and constrain possible 'individual' actions.

While discussion about commuting and global business travel has accepted that the demand for such travel is price inelastic, leisure travel and travel for social networking have been presumed to be price elastic. Leisure travel has often been seen as unnecessary and therefore price elastic. However, the respondents' accounts make it very clear that leisure travel is anything but unnecessary. It is central to their social lives and to the building and maintenance of their social capital, and of social capital more widely. We suspect then that this kind of travel is relatively price inelastic once certain novel patterns have been established, as through the use of the car and of budget air travel.

We have also seen just how empirically significant such travel is. Table 5 and Table 6 below show that leisure travel constitutes the most significant category of trips made and miles travelled in various industrialized societies (even allowing for the unsatisfactory nature of such classifications).

Table 5   Share of trips by trip purpose (%)

Trip purpose	Switzerland	Germany	UK	USA
Leisure	39.5	35.0	26.5	26.7
Work/School	35.5	18.2	25.3	25.2
Shopping/Private business	19.1	34.8	31.3	37.6
Escorting Others	4.8	6.4	12.6	10.2
Others	1.0	5.6	4.3	0.2
Total	100.0	100.0	100.0	100.0

Source: Bundesamt für Raumentwicklung (2000); Deutsches Institut für Wirtschaftsforschung (2003); DfT (2004); Bureau of Transportation Statistics (1995).

Table 6   Share of distance travelled by trip purpose (%)

Trip purpose	Switzerland	Germany	UK	USA
Leisure	44.8	38.3	33.7	32.2
Work/School	35.0	29.7	32.0	31.3
Shopping/Private business	11.2	21.7	19.7	27.6
Escort	4.9	4.5	7.6	8.5
Others	1.8	4.8	7.1	0.5
Total	100.0	100.0	100.0	100.0

Source: Bundesamt für Raumentwicklung (2000) ; Deutsches Institut für Wirtschaftsforschung (2003); DfT (2004); Bureau of Transportation Statistics (1995).

The research also brings out how business and leisure are not useful as exclusive categories when respondents are asked to classify their travel experience. Single journeys accommodate various purposes, so that an exclusive categorization becomes arbitrary and misleading: what, for example, is a business journey, so arranged as to permit employer-subsidized attendance at a family wedding?

We also found that respondents employ different modes of contacting, meeting and talking with their network members. The various forms of telecommunication are extensively employed to plan, coordinate, schedule, reschedule and debrief face-to-face meetings. Their usage is co-evolving into a situation where firm advance commitments to places, times and participants are often replaced by more fluid forms, in which the final group, place and time coalesce out of many short interactions: some involving whole groups through email or SMS texts, or of certain individuals through one-to-one exchanges of texts or phone calls.

We found many ways in which the respondents thus combine local contacts and faraway connections. The average distances to where significant others live are substantial and this is so across the three occupations. The distances are managed by combining mediated contacts (phone, SMS, email) with intermittent visits that tend to become rarer but also of longer duration as distances grow. Email use expands as distances increase. Overall it would seem that the size and the variance of the social network geographies have increased.

There are limitations of this research: first, the small sample size and our dependence on a sample willing to share their family and friendship secrets with us; second, the focus upon the individual and his/her networks rather than the examination of each network as a system; and third, the fact that the current scale of social network geographies cannot be judged by comparison with the past.

This lack of historical comparison makes it difficult to say if the growth of social networks is increasing, slowed or come to a standstill. One would expect that the process will follow a hysteresis-type pattern. Initially the process will be slow, as people restructure their social networks to reap the benefits of the lower generalized costs (that is, time, money and comfort). Given that personal social capital is embedded in these relationships one would not expect fast change. As the social capital encompasses both the joint history, commitments, references and understandings of the network members, as well as their joint ability to perform, act and enjoy, people will be loath to risk this too quickly. It is only after they have learnt that relationships can be retained and developed at the desired level of quality over a distance that the spatial growth process will start in earnest, as we have documented with these young people in this research. Travel becomes essential for the social capital of a given society. In cross-sectional analysis we would expect that there is an association of higher incomes or better access to the infrastructure networks with larger social network geographies.

Equally, if a network finds itself in a position of increasing generalized costs, if for example air duty was to be paid on airline flights or road charging became widespread, then we would expect an initially slow adjustment, which will only accelerate when the network cannot ignore the increased costs anymore. This hysteresis pattern should be observable over the life course of people and their networks, as normally incomes rise to some point, which makes travel and communication more affordable, but from some point both financial resources decrease and the ability to travel effortlessly declines.

Policy Implications

If we assume that the patterns identified in our sample of young adults, mostly before the child-rearing part of their life, will be maintained in at least an attenuated form, as well as spread more generally in the population, then transport policy has many challenges to face. Currently, these patterns are particularly prominent for respondents who had to move for education or training, but it is not limited to respondents with high-prestige jobs. The history of personal trainers in our research showed the significance of training on cruise ships and the importance of this experience for future networks. Furthermore, even people who themselves have not moved much beyond their place of birth can be part of such far-flung networks through relatives, friends or acquaintances who have moved or in some cases returned.

The research reported here changes our understanding of travel. Transport planning bases its analysis on individual utility maximizing agents, even if the analysis allows for some impacts of joint decision making within each household. These agents interact in markets and upon the infrastructures provided, operated or regulated by the state or private providers. The perspective of most planners is therefore focused on first, the traveller as an economic agent, working, shopping and consuming services, and second, on the demand peaks of the infrastructures that constrain the choices of the travellers and generate a large share of the externalities associated with travelling (Brilon, Geistefeldt and Zurlinden 2004). An alternative view arising from the research undertaken here sees the traveller as a network-based actor whose actions and choices are more often than not negotiated with personally significant third parties. These choices reflect the exchange processes typical of social networks and cannot therefore be well captured with the assumption of individual utility-maximizing behaviour.

Moreover, in traditional analysis leisure travel is seen as a minor residual category. Sometimes analysts even deploy moralistic terms, such as superfluous, voluntary or wasteful. It is clear, though, from this research that leisure travel is in most cases anything but inessential and will remain so as long as travellers need face-to-face contacts to build, maintain and develop their social networks and social capital.

The mapping of the social network geographies for the named contacts has demonstrated the spatial reach of these respondents. Even if we allow for the fact that our research instrument was only able to capture parts of the networks in the given time, it is noticeable that respondents in all occupation categories possessed strong long-distance links. The respondents do not live exclusively local lives. They mostly have national frames of references and some international frames.

A further topic we could not explore were the implications of these larger frames for the lived reality of local communities. Local residents who are often or even always absent might be expected to be less effective members of such communities (see Putnam 2000, for analysis of this 'crisis' of local communities; and see Chapter 2 above). The non-local lifestyles that this research reveals might link to the perceived crisis of the 'local'. The literature reflects a perceived lack of neighbourhood, but also a sense of physical insecurity (see Axhausen 2000). What has been termed *localized anomie* could be seen as a social consequence or externality of these distanciated social network geographies. Such busy travellers may then *as residents* spend significant resources to regain their feelings of security, through investing in additional alarm and safety installations, by moving to guarded environments, or by collectively supporting large systems of video surveillance within the public domain, developing what Diken and Laustsen term new kinds of 'camp' (2005). Further research would also examine to what extent the weakness of local democracy is a result of many people living these significantly non-local lives, and then developing various camps and gates in order to 'secure' themselves.

Overall, the patterns we discovered are likely to be typical of a trend towards larger and continuously growing network geographies. This assumed trend is in line with result of mainstream transport policy: improvement of accessibility through lower generalized costs of travel, in particular higher speeds, while controlling and limiting the externalities of travel. For a continuation of this policy our results would not suggest major changes. A further reduction of the generalized cost of travel will allow travellers to expand their geographies even further. Given their interest in fast and reliable travel for their frequent, if time-constraint weekend journeys, such travellers will have a higher than usual willingness to pay for reliability and speed even if airlines had, for example, to charge duty on their fuel (that is, inelastic demand).

If transport policy were developed to control the environmental externalities of travel and the social externalities suggested above, then this research reveals many hurdles to policy implementation that an economic and engineering analysis would not. Such a trend-reversing policy would have to increase the generalized costs of travel either directly through higher taxes, rationing or lower speeds, or indirectly through higher capital requirements for private vehicles matching more demanding technical specifications.[1] The initial hurdle is that the population might not be willing to support such a trend-reversing policy in the first place. Beyond resentment against increased and maybe uncompensated higher monetary costs of travel, many will see the negative implications of such changes for its very patterning of social life and social capital. As any reconstruction of this social capital is anxiety inducing, costly and time consuming, people would need to be offered a very convincing case for such a transformation away from current increasingly path-dependent patterns of social networking conducted at-a-distance.

The speed of implementation would be crucial here. A policy of sustained generalized cost increase for private transport would need to be accompanied by a regulatory framework generating fast, reliable, comfortable and affordable public transport services that are spatially widespread and as effective as the car in sustaining this complexly rich and networked form of life. Flexibility is a key notion here as revealed by this research. Public transport would have to be *as flexible as* the

---

1   At this time all alternative technologies discussed to reduce emissions will increase the costs of a like-for-like car. It is clear that the travellers can compensate here by choosing smaller or less well-specified cars.

car with regard to information, pricing, routing-ticketing, multi-trips, multimember journey groups, comfort, fashionability and the carrying of luggage/bags (see Urry 2004c; Foresight Directorate 2006). The current practice of reducing service levels at weekends and Sunday engineering works on UK railways would need to be entirely rethought!

Such a policy would also need to explore the contribution of information and communications technology-mediated communications in this reconstruction. Such communications can replace some journeys and therefore this could reduce the regularity of contact. This will be especially important if the richness of the senses encountered face-to-face can be effectively simulated through skyping, webcams and videoconferencing features likely to develop over the next decade or so (see Foresight Directorate 2006).

The research also showed how journeys often fulfil various purposes, including family life, business, sightseeing, socializing among colleagues and meeting local social contacts. This opens up new opportunities for tourism policy. On the one hand, the pricing structures and services of hotels and local transportation providers should cater for these multifaceted visits, while on the other hand tourism policy statistics should seek to capture, measure and map these currently mostly privately accommodated visits more effectively (certainly by avoiding simple exclusive categories). Dienel, Meier-Dallach and Schröder (2004) even suggest that one should link visitors and locals socially, so as to increase the attraction of particular destinations. While this often happens already, as owners and staff develop relationships with regulars, one could give these processes more attention and support.

This book has not much explored how social exclusion fits into its explanatory scheme except to point to the centrality of the concept of network capital. Future work would need to address this further (see Cass, Shove and Urry 2003, 2005). Social exclusion, we would suggest, results for those groups whose social networks are closed and which do not provide (enough) links to the outside social world. As a result of the limited network capital such groups find their resources are not strong enough to provide an appropriate style of life, so resulting in precarious lives dependent upon state or voluntary help. The greater the significance of new forms of network capital, the more it is necessary to access such capital even to stay in the same position so as to share an appropriately dignified life.

Research Implications

Neither transport nor sociological research has in the past examined the links we have established between social networks, location and travel. Past benchmarks or longitudinal observations are therefore missing. From our perspective it seems necessary to fill this gap through new survey work. Two sets of items would be important: first, those capturing the social content of activities and of their participants, and second, those describing the social network geographies.

First, the social content of an activity has many layers, which will differ for the various participants of an activity. The following items would be essential to identify and measure:

- A more detailed coding of activity, maybe at the level of detail typical for time-use studies;
- A description of the social purpose of the activity and of the obligations fulfilled with it;
- Composition of the party travelling together to the activity;
- Composition of the party participating in the event(s) and having meaningful interactions with the respondent;
- Home locations of the fellow travellers and participants, or alternatively their location prior to the trip or activity;
- Distribution of the travel and activity costs among the participants and beneficiaries;
- The planning horizon of the activity;
- The secondary activities undertaken during the trip and the activity, if any;
- The forms of network capital possessed by each respondent.[2]

Second, the items in the interviews that we conducted relating to respondents' social networks and the frequency and location of contacts should be included in any larger-scale survey:

- List of relevant contacts and their home locations;
- Frequency of contact by mode (face-to-face, email, phone, SMS, letter, chat etc.);
- Location of face-to-face meetings;
- Nature of the location of such meetings.

The required benchmarking will aim to draw representative samples to allow the characterization of the current situation and later the determination of trends. Nevertheless, certain groups deserve special attention, as they either contribute disproportionate shares of the total mileage travelled, or because they are deemed to be at risk of social exclusion. The following types are in the first category and should be especially researched: household and families divided between different locations for the bulk of the time (for example, couples regularly working/living in different towns); parent with children boarding away for their education; households regularly circulating between different locations (for example, the switch between a pied-à-terre in town and a home in the country); long-term stays at holiday homes in the UK or abroad; migrant families and their travel to the place where the parental

---

2   Individual items in this list have been included in diary surveys elsewhere but their final form would need to be developed in a series of tests. (See Axhausen et al 2002; Schlich, Simma and Axhausen 2003; Axhausen 2005a; Löchl et al 2005.)

generation grew up; migrant families travelling to the location that defines the post-migration centre of gravity of their networks, if they live away from it; and diasporic families returning to the ancestral country of origin.

One set of examples that could be researched are festivals such as Dewali for Indians, Thanksgiving for US Americans, and also the annual fair that reunites people from the same village or town. This would enable one to see how the social networks at the different places shape the travel of the groups with respect to timing, duration and form.

Moreover, the emphasis on the social context and content of travel should not lead to the conclusion that travellers do not sometimes travel alone. To be able to assess the size of the social network geographies and of their impacts it will be necessary to capture the complete activity space of travellers, with others and on their own. The methods for this are available, as demonstrated by various long-duration travel diaries (Schönfelder and Axhausen 2003, 2004), as well as by long-duration observations with GPS-based data.

Conclusion

We have thus sought to integrate social network analysis into the study of travel and transport and have developed some theories and methods to advance this integration. To develop this integration further some more questions should be asked. First, is it possible to obtain valid information on social network geographies from large representative samples or should such research concentrate upon the small sample model we have deployed in this book? Second, just what is the social content of the various activities that are undertaken by people when they 'meet' together and how significant are they in establishing and maintaining social networks? Indeed, how strongly does the social content of an activity explain the form of the related journey undertaken (through timing, mode, location)? Is there a link between the social network geographies we have analysed and the forms of what we refer to in this chapter as local anomie? Is it possible to model these processes efficiently and reliably in microsimulation models of travel demand? And most significantly, how can these complex socialities and geographies that seem from this small study of young adults in the North-West of England to be irreversible be supported by future transport and communications technologies in ways that are much less environmentally harmful?

Appendix A

Distances To and Locations of Significant Others

Table 7   **Distances to significant others**

Interviewee	Number of non-local friends named	Mean distance to non-local friends	Number of family members named	Mean distance to family members			Number of most-important people named	Mean distance to persons named most important		
				to all	to all but the one furthest away	to all but the one living closest		to all	to the closest three	to the furthest three
No. 14	4	4336	3	29	29	29	10	1712	0	5687
No. 22	6	4144	5	424	90	530	N/A	N/A	N/A	N/A
No. 18	5	3752	4	56	56	56	7	2652	19	6148
No. 12	9	3090	3	350	350	350	7	1273	75	2819
No. 24	6	2889	3	3401	132	5094	9	93	2	185
No. 23	3	2672	3	31	31	31	7	22	10	31
No. 9	6	1750	4	2672	340	3496	6	160	59	262
No. 5	10	1697	4	203	203	203	7	115	12	234
No. 4	9	1677	3	108	0	162	10	1484	0	4715
No. 2	10	1607	3	3679	3679	3679	N/A	N/A	N/A	N/A
No. 8	10	1341	N/A	N/A	N/A	N/A	9	246	58	477
No. 16	7	1103	4	69	61	71	5	48	20	80
No. 10	6	826	3	267	267	267	9	447	0	1013
No. 13	10	702	5	146	117	154	8	88	39	117

Table 7 Continued

Interviewee	Number of non-local friends named	Mean distance to non-local friends	Number of family members named	Mean distance to family members			Number of most-important people named	Mean distance to persons named most important		
				to all	to all but the one furthest away	to all but the one living closest		to all	to the closest three	to the furthest three
No. 1	8	383	6	17	0	21	8	13	0	35
No. 6	6	375	5	35	27	44	6	27	0	54
No. 7	8	349	5	333	170	381	5	38	11	58
No. 21	8	203	7	1194	14	1394	10	19	0	39
No. 3	7	185	4	94	83	99	9	95	31	168
No. 15	5	144	4	1426	0	1901	10	61	0	187
No. 19	6	125	8	888	38	1015	10	47	0	146
No. 17	1	94	5	0	0	0	10	14	0	39
No. 11	3	60	4	57	57	57	9	27	0	61
No. 20	3	41	7	457	25	533	10	14	0	44
Mean of mean	6.50	1398	4.43	693	251	851	8.23	395	15	1027

Table 8   Location of significant others

Inter-viewee	*Non-local friends* Home location	*Great-circle distance*	*Family members* Home location	*Great-circle distance*	*Most important persons* Home location	*Great-circle distance*
No. 1	**Mean**	**383**	**Mean**	**17**	**Mean**	**13**
	Munich	1176	Leeds	103	Manchester	53
	Cologne	731	Liverpool	0	Manchester	53
	London	289	Liverpool	0	Liverpool	0
	Reading	258	Liverpool	0	Liverpool	0
	Bath	230	Liverpool	0	Liverpool	0
	Grantham	168	Liverpool	0	Liverpool	0
	Darlington	156			Liverpool	0
	Manchester	53			Liverpool	0
No. 2	**Mean**	**1607**	**Mean**	**3679**		
	Chicago	5695	Ufa	3679		
	Haifa	3814	Ufa	3679		
	Moscow	2536	Ufa	3679		
	Rome	1687				
	Berlin	1047				
	Essen	664				
	Glasgow	290				
	London	264				
	Formby	53				
	Bolton	17				
No. 3	**Mean**	**185**	**Mean**	**94**	**Mean**	**95**
	Brighton	346	Birmingham	128	Croydon	299
	Portsmouth	322	Telford	89	Leeds	103
	London	289	Shrewsbury	80	Leeds	103
	Birmingham	128	Shrewsbury	80	Telford	89
	Leeds	103			Telford	89
	Shrewsbury	80			Telford	89
	Chester	24			Shrewsbury	80
					Shrewsbury	80
					Prescott	13
					Liverpool	0

Table 8   Continued

Inter-viewee	Non-local friends		Family members		Most important persons	
	Home location	Great-circle distance	Home location	Great-circle distance	Home location	Great-circle distance
No. 4	**Mean**	**1677**	**Mean**	**108**	**Mean**	**1484**
	Mauritius	10026	Dorking	323	Mauritius	10026
	Egypt	3797	Southport	0	Egypt	3797
	Brighton	369	Southport	0	Dorking	323
	London	309			London	309
	Glasgow	254			Glasgow	254
	Birmingham	152			Sheffield	105
	Sheffield	105			Liverpool	28
	Manchester	55			Southport	0
	Liverpool	28			Southport	0
					Southport	0
No. 5	**Mean**	**1697**	**Mean**	**203**	**Mean**	**115**
	Mexico City	8662	Ireland	203	London	295
	Dubai	5706	Ireland	203	Dublin	203
	Germany	1112	Ireland	203	Dublin	203
	Limerick	372	Ireland	203	Manchester	66
	London	295			Liverpool	12
	Edinburgh	286			Liverpool	12
	Cardiff	209			Wirral	12
	Dublin	203				
	Manchester	66				
	Bangor	63				
No. 6	**Mean**	**375**	**Mean**	**35**	**Mean**	**27**
	Spain	1460	Blackpool	65	Coventry	129
	Ireland	268	Blackpool	65	Huddersfield	33
	Suffolk	256	Wigan	27	Manchester	0
	Leamington Spa	141	Bolton	17	Manchester	0
	Nottingham	92	Manchester	0	Manchester	0
	Huddersfield	33			Manchester	0

Table 8 **Continued**

Inter-viewee	Non-local friends		Family members		Most important persons	
	Home location	Great-circle distance	Home location	Great-circle distance	Home location	Great-circle distance
No. 7	**Mean**	**349**	**Mean**	**333**	**Mean**	**38**
	Berlin	1106	Basel	986	Wootton Wawen	145
	Basel	986	Reading	249	Liverpool	15
	Milton Keynes	212	Wootton Wawen	145	Liverpool	15
	Cardiff	198	Wootten Wawen	145	Hoylake	13
	Wootton Wawen	145	Coventry	141	Heswall	4
	Leeds	115				
	Liverpool	15				
	Chester	14				
No. 8	**Mean**	**1341**			**Mean**	**246**
	Cape Town	9920			Aaachen	687
	Copenhagen	1033			Bonallack	400
	Aachen	687			Plymouth	343
	Falmouth	389			London	289
	Plymouth	343			Strafford u. Avon	162
	Helensborough	310			Leamington Spa	158
	London	289			Warwick	158
	Belfast	231			Parkgate	15
	Leamington Spa	158			Liverpool	0
	Manchester	53				
No. 9	**Mean**	**1750**	**Mean**	**2672**	**Mean**	**160**
	Hong Kong	9665	Hong Kong	9665	London	289
	London	289	Brussels	576	Cambridge	248
	Cambridge	248	Cambridge	248	Cambridge	248
	Nottingham	132	Sunderland	197	Durham	177
	Wales	114			Liverpool	0
	Manchester	53			Liverpool	0

Table 8   Continued

Inter-viewee	Non-local friends		Family members		Most important persons	
	Home location	Great-circle distance	Home location	Great-circle distance	Home location	Great-circle distance
No.10	**Mean**	**826**	**Mean**	**267**	**Mean**	**447**
	Portugal	1726	Southend	267	Portugal	1726
	Barcelona	1386	Southend	267	Berlin	1047
	Berlin	1047	Southend	267	Essex	267
	Ireland	268			Essex	267
	Essex	267			Essex	267
	London	264			Manchester	0
					Manchester	0
					Manchester	0
No. 11	**Mean**	**60**	**Mean**	**57**	**Mean**	**27**
	Harrogate	70	Chester	57	Harrogate	70
	Chester	57	Chester	57	Chester	57
	Leeds	53	Chester	57	Chester	57
			Chester	57	Chester	57
					Manchester	0
					Manchester	0
					Manchester	0
					Manchester	0
					Manchester	0
No. 12	**Mean**	**3090**	**Mean**	**350**	**Mean**	**1273**
	New Zealand	18625	South Devon	350	Tanzania	7743
	Tanzania	7743	South Devon	350	Totnes	357
	Plymouth	368	South Devon	350	Totnes	357
	Southampton	294			St Albans	232
	Essex	267			Co. Durham	146
	St Albans	232			Derby	79
	Co. Durham	146			Manchester	0
	Derby	79				
	Leeds	53				

Table 8   Continued

Inter-viewee	Non-local friends		Family members		Most important persons	
	Home location	Great-circle distance	Home location	Great-circle distance	Home location	Great-circle distance
No. 13	**Mean**	**702**	**Mean**	**146**	**Mean**	**88**
	America	5695	London	264	Birmingham	117
	Scotland	280	Leicester	117	Leicester	117
	London	264	Leicester	117	Leicester	117
	Bridlington Ton	147	Leicester	117	Leicester	117
	Coventry	129	Leicester	117	Leicester	117
	Hull	126			Leicester	117
	Birmingham	117			Manchester	0
	Leicester	117			Manchester	0
	Nottingham	92				
	Sheffield	50				
No. 14	**Mean**	**4336**	**Mean**	**29**	**Mean**	**1712**
	Australia	16997	Warrington	29	Australia	16997
	London	264	Warrington	29	Altrincuar	34
	Leeds	53	Warrington	29	Warrington	29
	Warrington	29			Warrington	29
					Warrington	29
					Manchester	0
					Manchester	0
					Manchester	0
					Manchester	0
					Manchester	0
No. 15	**Mean**	**144**	**Mean**	**1425**	**Mean**	**187**
	Felixstowe	285	America	5702	Felixstowe	285
	London	252	Stockport	0	London	252
	Leicester	106	Stockport	0	Bury	24
	Matlock Bath	51	Stockport	0	Macclesfield	17
	Bury	24			Manchester	12
					Ashton u. Lyne	12
					Reddish	3
					Stockport	0
					Stockport	0
					Stockport	0

Table 8 **Continued**

Inter- viewee	Non-local friends		Family members		Most important persons	
	Home location	*Great- circle distance*	*Home location*	*Great- circle distance*	*Home location*	*Great- circle distance*
No. 16	**Mean**	**1103**	**Mean**	**69**	**Mean**	**48**
	Miami	6949	Nottingham	92	Burton	110
	London	264	Matlock	61	Uttoxeter	71
	Oxford	205	Matlock	61	Chesterfield	60
	Burton	110	Matlock	61	Manchester	0
	Uttoxeter	71			Manchester	0
	Matlock	61				
	Chesterfield	60				
No 17	**Mean**	**94**	**Mean**	**0**	**Mean**	**14**
			Stockport	0	York	94
			Stockport	0	Manchester	12
			Stockport	0	Manchester	12
			Stockport	0	Manchester	12
			Stockport	0	Manchester	12
					Stockport	0
					Stockport	0
					Stockport	0
					Stockport	0
					Stockport	0
No. 18	**Mean**	**3752**	**Mean**	**56**	**Mean**	**2652**
	Miami	6949	Wirral	56	Miami	6949
	Chicago	6127	Wirral	56	Chicago	6127
	New York	5368	Wirral	56	New York	5368
	London	264	Wirral	56	Little Neston	61
	Liverpool	53			Wirral	56
					Manchester	0
					Manchester	0

Table 8   Continued

Inter-viewee	Non-local friends		Family members		Most important persons	
	Home location	Great-circle distance	Home location	Great-circle distance	Home location	Great-circle distance
No. 19	**Mean**	**126**	**Mean**	**888**	**Mean**	**47**
	London	338	India	6837	London	338
	Leicester	191	Leicester	191	Bolton	59
	Dewsbury	89	Blackburn	41	Blackburn	41
	Bolton	59	Preston	34	Preston	34
	Blackburn	41	Lancaster	0	Lancaster	0
	Preston	34	Lancaster	0	Lancaster	0
			Lancaster	0	Lancaster	0
			Lancaster	0	Lancaster	0
					Lancaster	0
					Lancaster	0
No. 20	**Mean**	**41**	**Mean**	**457**	**Mean**	**14**
	York	115	Tenerife	3046	York	115
	Heysham	6	Birslems Pottery's	148	Dolphine-holme	11
	Morecambe	1	Morecambe	1	Heysham	6
			Morecambe	1	Morecambe	1
			Lancaster	0	Morecambe	1
			Lancaster	0	Morecambe	1
			Lancaster	0	Lancaster	0
					Lancaster	0
					Lancaster	0
					Lancaster	0
No. 21	**Mean**	**203**	**Mean**	**1194**	**Mean**	**19**
	Nice	1365	San Francisco	8280	Southport	46
	Stockport	87	Southport	46	Preston	35
	Manchester	75	Preston	35	Preston	35
	Southport	46	Morecambe	0	Preston	35
	Preston	35	Morecambe	0	Preston	35
	Carnforth	8	Morecambe	0	Carnforth	8
	Carnforth	8	Morecambe	0	Lancaster	1
	Lancaster	1			Lancaster	1
					Morecambe	0
					Morecambe	0

Table 8   Continued

Inter-viewee	Non-local friends Home location	Great-circle distance	Family members Home location	Great-circle distance	Most important persons Home location	Great-circle distance
No. 22	**Mean**	**4144**	**Mean**	**424**		
	Australia	16998	Italy	1759		
	America	5639	Derby	153		
	Italy	1759	Derby	153		
	London	338	Rawtenstall	54		
	Manchester	74	Lancaster	0		
	Rawtenstall	54				
No. 23	**Mean**	**2672**	**Mean**	**31**	**Mean**	**22**
	Tanzania	7816	Blackpool	31	Blackpool	31
	Hull	168	Blackpool	31	Blackpool	31
	Blackpool	31	Blackpool	31	Blackpool	31
			Blackpool	31	Blackpool	31
					Blackpool	31
					Lancaster	0
					Lancaster	0
No.24	**Mean**	**2889**	**Mean**	**3401**	**Mean**	**93**
	Cape Town	9941	Cape Town	9941	London	291
	Canada	5119	Didcot	247	Didcot	247
	Stockholm	1397	Lonsridse	16	Lonsridse	16
	Bournemouth	335			Blackburn	6
	London	291			Darwen	0
	Bristol	250			Darwen	0

Appendix B

Distribution of Distances by Rank

One can extend the analysis of the distances between the respondents and their most important contacts by dividing the contacts into groups depending on the distance between them and the respondent. Figure 3 shows means and the associated 95 per cent confidence intervals of four groups. The first group represents the closest 25 per cent of contacts, the first 50 per cent and so on. For each respondent and portion a mean was calculated. The means of these means are displayed. It is clearly visible that the nearest of the most important contacts are local and that distance grows only afterwards. Our respondents clearly combine local and distant friends to constitute their circle of friends.

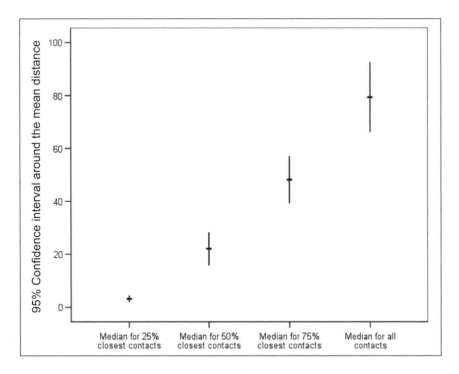

Figure 3   **Mean distance and 95 per cent confidence interval to most important contacts sorted by their distance from the respondent**

References

Adams, J. (1999), *The Social Implications of Hybermobility, OECD Project on Environmentally Sustainable Transport* (London: UCL) http://www.geog.ucl. ac.uk/~jadams/publish.htm, accessed 5 February 2006.

Ahmed, S., Castañeda, C., Fortier, A. and Sheller, M. (eds) (2003), *Uprootings/ Regroundings: Questions of Home and Migration* (Oxford: Berg).

Albrow, M. (1997), 'Travelling Beyond Local Cultures: Socioscapes in a Global City', in J. Eade (ed.) *Living the Global City: Globalization as Local Process* (London: Routledge).

Albrow, M., Eade, J., Durrschmidt, J. and Washbourne, N. (eds) (1997), 'The Impact of Globalization on Sociological Concepts: Community, Culture and Milieu', in J. Eade (ed.) *Living the Global City: Globalization as Local Process* (London: Routledge).

Allan, G. and Crow, G. (eds) (2001), *Families, Households and Society* (Basingstoke: Palgrave).

Allen, J. (2000), 'On George Simmel: Proximity, Distance and Movement', in M. Crang and N. Thrift (eds) *Thinking Space* (London: Routledge).

Appadurai, A. (1988), 'Putting Hierarchy in its Place', *Cultural Anthropology*, 3:1, 36–49.

Axhausen, K.W. (2000), 'Geographies of Somewhere: A Review of Urban Literature', *Urban Studies* 37:10, 1849–64.

—— (2005a), 'Activity Spaces, Biographies, Social Networks and their Welfare Gains and Externalities: Some Hypotheses and Empirical Results', paper given to the PROCESSUS Colloquium, Toronto.

—— (2005b), 'Social Networks and Travel: Some Hypotheses', in K. Donaghy, S. Poppelreuter and G. Rudinger (eds) *Social Aspects of Sustainable Transport: Transatlantic Perspectives* (Aldershot: Ashgate).

——, Zimmerman, A., Schönfelder, S., Rindsfuser, G. and Haupt, T. (2002), 'Observing the Rhythms of Daily Life: A Six-week Travel Diary', *Transportation* 29:2, 95–124.

—— and Fröhlich, P. (2004), 'Public Investment and Accessibility Change', in H. Held and P. Marti (eds) *Bauen, Bewirtschaften, Erneuern – Gedanken zur Gestaltung der Infrastruktur* (Zurich: IVT, ETH).

——, Sigrun, B., Bernard, M., Fröhlich, P., Jermann, J. and Vrtic, M. (2004), *Perspektiven des Schweizerischen Verkehrs bis 2030: Module M04 und M05 Besitz von Mobilitätswerkzeugen – Fahrleistungen/Betriebsleistungen und Verkehrsleistungen, Bericht an das ARE* (Zurich: IVT, ETH).

Bachen, C. (2001), 'The Family in the Networked Society: A Summary of Research on the American Family', http://sts.scu.edu/nexus/Issue1-1/Bachen_TheNetworkedFamily.asp, accessed 31 November 2004.

Bærenholdt, J.O., Haldrup, M., Larsen, J. and Urry, J. (2004), *Performing Tourist Places* (Aldershot: Ashgate).

Baldassar, L. (2001), *Visits Home: Migration Experiences between Italy and Australia* (Melbourne: Melbourne University).

Barabàsi, A-L. (2002), *Linked: The New Science of Networks* (New York: Perseus Books Group).

Bartlett, R. (1993), *The Making of Europe: Conquest, Colonization, and Cultural Change, 950–1350*. (Princeton: Princeton University Press).

Bauman, Z. (1998), *Globalization: The Human Consequences* (Cambridge: Polity Press).

—— (2000a), *Liquid Modernity* (Cambridge: Polity Press).

—— (2000b), 'Time and Space Reunited', *Time and Society* 9:2/3, 171–85.

—— (2003), *Liquid Love* (Cambridge: Polity Press).

Beaverstock, J. (2005), 'Transnational Elites in the City: British Highly-Skilled Transferees in New York's Financial District', *Journal of Ethnic and Migration Studies* 31:2, 245–69.

Beck, U. (2001), 'Living Your Own Life in a Runaway World: Individualisation, Globalization and Politics', in W. Hutton and A. Giddens (eds) *On the Edge: Living with Global Capitalism* (London: Vintage).

—— and Beck-Gernsheim, E. (1995), *The Normal Chaos of Love* (Cambridge: Polity Press).

Beck-Gernsheim, E. (2002), *Reinventing the Family: in Search of New Lifestyles* (London: Blackwell).

Bell, C. and Newby, H. (1976), 'Communion, Communalism, Class and Community Action: The Sources of New Urban Politics', in D. Herbert and R. Johnston (eds) *Social Areas in Cities, Volume 2* (Chichester: Wiley).

Boase, J. and Wellman, B. (2004), 'Personal Relationships: On and Off the Internet', in A. Vangelisti and D. Perlman (eds) *Cambridge Handbook of Personal Relationships* (Cambridge: Cambridge University Press).

Boden, D. (1994), *The Business of Talk: Organisations in Action* (Cambridge: Polity Press).

—— (2000), 'Worlds in Action: Information, Instantaneity and Global Futures Trading', in B. Adam, U. Beck and J. Van Loon (eds) *The Risk Society and Beyond: Critical Issues for Social Theory* (London: Sage).

—— and Molotch, H. (1994), 'The Compulsion of Proximity', in R. Friedland and D. Boden (eds) *Nowhere: Space, Time and Modernity* (Berkeley: University of California Press).

de Botton, A. (2002), *The Art of Travel* (New York: Pantheon Books).

Bourdieu, P. (1984), *Distinction: A Social Critique of the Judgment of Taste* (London: Routledge and Kegan Paul).

Brilon, W., Geistefeldt, J. and Zurlinden, H. (2004), 'Ganzjahresanalyse des Verkehrsflusses auf Autobahnen', *Strassenverkehrstechnik* 48:11, 595–600.

Brown, B. (2002), 'Studying the Use of Mobile Technology', in B. Brown, N. Green, and R. Harper (eds) *Wireless World: Social and Interactional Aspects of the Mobile Age* (London: Springer).

—— and O'Hara, K. (2003), 'Place as a Practical Concern of Mobile Workers', *Environment and Planning A* 35, 1565–87.

Buchanan, M. (2002), *Nexus: Small Worlds and the Groundbreaking Science of Networks* (London: W.W. Norton).

Bundesamt für Raumentwicklung (2000), *Mikrozensus zum Verkehrsverhalten 2000*, http://www.are.admin.ch/imperia/md/content/are/gesamtverkehr/verkehrs forschung2/25.xls, accessed September 2005.

Bureau of Transportation Statistics (1995), *Nationwide Personal Transportation Survey 1995*, http://www.transtats.bts.gov/DL_SelectFields.asp?Table_ID=1036 &DB_Short_Name=NPTS, accessed September 2005.

Byam, K.N. Zhang, Y. and Lin, M. (2004), 'Social Interactions across Media', *New Media and Society* 6:3, 299–318.

Cairncross, F. (1997), *The Death of Distance* (London: Orion Business Books).

Cairns, S., Sloman, L., Newson, C., Anable, J., Kirkbride, A. and Goodwin, P. (2004), *Smarter Choices – Changing the Way We Travel* (London: Department of Transport).

Caletrio, J. (2003), 'A Ravaging Mediterranean Passion: Tourism and Environmental Change in Europe's Playground', unpublished PhD thesis (Lancaster University: Department of Sociology).

Callon, M. and Law, J. (2004), 'Guest Editorial', *Environment and Planning D* 22, 3–11.

Cass, N., Shove, E. and Urry, J. (2003), 'Changing Infrastructures, Measuring Socio-spatial Inclusion', report for DfT (Lancaster University: Department of Sociology).

—— (2005), 'Social Exclusion, Mobility and Access', *Sociological Review* 53:3, 539–55.

Castells, M. (1996), *The Rise of the Network Society* (London: Blackwell).

—— (2000), 'Materials for an Explanatory Theory of the Network Society', *British Journal of Sociology* 51, 5–24.

—— (2001), *The Internet Galaxy: Reflections on the Internet, Business and Society* (Oxford: Oxford University Press).

Chamberlain, M. (1995), 'Family Narratives and Migration Dynamics', *Immigrants and Minorities* 14:2, 153–69.

Clifford, J. (1997), *Routes* (Cambridge, MA: Harvard University Press).

Cohen, E. (1972), 'Toward a Sociology of International Consumption', *Social Research* 39:1, 164–89.

Coleman, S. and Crang, M. (eds) (2002), *Tourism: Between Place and Performance* (Oxford: Berghahn Books).

Coles, T. and Timothy, D. (eds) (2004), *Tourism, Diasporas and Space* (London: Routledge).

——, Duvall, T. and Hall, C.M. (2005), 'Mobilising Tourism: A Post-Disciplinary Critique', *Tourism Recreation Research* 30:2, 31–41.

Collis, R. (2000), *The Survivor's Guide to Business Travel* (Dover: Herald International Tribune).

Condon, S.A. and Ogden, P.E. (1996), 'Questions of Emigration, Circulation and Return: Mobility between the French Caribbean and France', *International Journal of Population Geography* 2:1, 35–50.

Conradson, D. and Latham, A. (2005a), 'Friendship, Networks and Transnationality in a World City: Antipodean Transmigrants in London', *Journal of Ethnic and Migration Studies* 31:2, 287–305.

—— (2005b), 'Transnational Urbanism: Attending to Everyday Practices and Mobilities', *Journal of Ethnic and Migration Studies* 31:2, 227–33.

Couldry, N. (2005), 'On the Actual Street', in D. Crouch, R. Jackson and F. Thompson (eds) *The Media and The Tourist Imagination: Converging Cultures* (London: Routledge).

Cresswell, T. (2001), 'The Production of Mobilities', *New Formations* 43, 11–25.

—— (2002), *Mobilizing Place, Placing Mobility: The Politics of Representation in a Globalized World* (Amsterdam: Rodopi).

Crouch, D. Jackson, R. and Thompson, F. (eds) (2005), *The Media and the Tourist Imagination: Converging Cultures* (London: Routledge).

Dateline (2003), *Design and Application of a Travel Survey for European Long-distance trips based on an International Network of Expertise* (Munich: Institut für Verkehrs- und Infrastrukturforschung GmbH), http://www.ncl.ac.uk/dateline/home_page.htm, accessed 20 January 2006.

Davidson, R. and Cope, B. (2003), *Business Travel: Conferences, Incentive Travel, Exhibitions, Corporate Hospitality and Corporate Travel* (London: Prentice Hall).

De Vries, J. and Van Der Woude, A. (1997), *The First Modern Economy: Success, Failure, and Perseverance of the Dutch Economy, 1500–1815* (Cambridge: Cambridge University Press).

Department of Transport (2004), *National Travel Survey 2004*, http://www.dft.gov.uk/stellent/groups/dft_transstats/documents/page/dft_transstats_039328.xls, accessed September 2005.

Deutsches Institut für Wirtschaftsforschung (2003), *Mobilität in Deutschland 2003*, http://www.kontiv2002.de/pdf/mid2002_tabellenband_basis.pdf, accessed September 2005.

DfT (2004), *Transport Statistics Bulletin: National Travel Survey: 2003 – Final Results* (London: Department for Transport).

Dienel, L., Meier-Dallach, P.H. and Schröder, C. (eds) (2004), *Die neue Nähe: Raumpartnerschaften verbinden Kontrasträume* (Wiesbaden: Franz Steiner Verlag).

Diken, B. and Laustsen, C. (2005), *The Culture of Exception: Sociology Facing the Camp* (London: Routledge).

Dodds, P., Muhamad, R. and Duncan J.W. (2003), 'An Experimental Study of Search in Global Social Networks', *Science* 301:8, 827–9.

Donovan, N. Pilch, T. and Rubenstein, T. (2002), *Geographic Mobility* (London: Performance and Innovation Unit), http://www.strategy.gov.uk/downloads/su/gmseminar/gm_analytical.pdf, accessed 15 November 2004.

Doyle, J. and Nathan, M. (2001), *Wherever Next: Work in a Mobile World* (London: The Industrial Society).

Durrschmidt, J. (1997), 'Delinking of Locale and Milieu: on the Situatedness of Extended Milieus in a Global Environment', in J. Eade (ed.) *Living the Global City: Globalization as Local Process* (London: Routledge).

Duval, T.Y. (2004a), 'Conceptualising Return Visits: a Transnational Perspective', in T. Coles and T. Dallen (eds) *Tourism, Diasporas and Space* (London: Routledge).

—— (2004b), 'Linking Return Visits and Return Migration among Commonwealth Eastern Caribbean Migrants in Toronto', *Global Networks* 4, 51–8.

Edensor, T. (2000), 'Staging Tourism: Tourists as Performers', *Annals of Tourism Research* 27, 322–44.

Ellegård, K. and Vilhelmson, B. (2004), 'Home as a Pocket of Local Order: Everyday Activities and the Friction of Distance', *Geografiska Annaler Series B* 86:4, 281–96.

Featherstone, M., Thift, N. and Urry, J. (eds) (2005), *Automobilities* (London: Sage).

Fennel, G. (1997), 'Local Lives – Distant Ties: Researching Communities under Globalized Conditions', in J. Eade (ed.) *Living the Global City: Globalization as Local Process* (London: Routledge).

Florida, R. (2002), *The Rise of the Creative Class* (New York: Basic Books).

Foresight Directorate (2006), *Intelligent Information Futures. Project Overview* (London: Department for Trade and Industry).

Fortunati, L. (2005), 'Is the Body-to-Body Communication Still the Prototype?', *The Information Society* 21, 53–61.

Fox, K. (2001), *Evolution, Alienation and Gossip: The Role of Mobile Telecommunications in the 21st Century* (Oxford: Social Issues Research Centre), http://www.sirc.org/publik/gossip.shtml, accessed 18 February 2005.

Franklin, A. (2003), *Tourism: An Introduction* (London: Sage).

—— and Crang, M. (2001), 'The Trouble with Tourism and Travel Theory', *Tourist Studies* 1:1, 5–22.

Frändberg, L. and Vilhelmson, B. (2003), 'Personal Mobility: A Corporeal Dimension of Transnationalisation: The Case of Long-distance Travel from Sweden', *Environment and Planning A* 35, 1751–68.

Gans, H. (1962), *The Urban Villagers: Group and Class in the Life of Italian-Americans* (New York: Free Press of Glencoe).

Gergen, K. (2002), 'The Challenge of Absent Presence', in J. Katz and M. Aakhus (eds) *Perpetual Contact: Mobile Communication, Private Talk, Public Performance* (Cambridge: Cambridge University Press).

Geser, H. (2004), *Towards a Sociological Theory of the Mobile Phone* (Zurich: University of Zurich, http://socio.ch/mobile/t_geser1.htm, accessed 10 March 2006.

Gibson, J.J. (1979), *The Ecological Approach to Visual Perception* (Boston: Houghton Mifflin).

Giddens, A. (1992), *The Transformation of Intimacy* (Cambridge: Polity Press).

—— (1994), 'Living in a Post-traditional Society', in U. Bech, A. Giddens and S. Lash (eds) *Reflexive Modernization: Politics, Tradition and Aesthetics* (London: Routledge).

Gillespie, A. and Richardson, R. (2004), 'Teleworking and the City: Myths of Workplace Transcendence and Travel Reduction', in S. Graham (ed.) *The Cybercities Reader* (London: Routledge).

Golob, F.T. and Regan, A.C. (2001), 'Impacts of Information Technology on Personal Travel and Commercial Vehicle Operations: Research Challenges and Opportunities', *Transportation Research Part C* 9, 87–121.

Gordon, D., Adelman, L., Ashworth, K., Bradshaw, J., Levitas, R., Middleton, S., Pantazis, C., Patsios, D., Payne, S., Townsend, P., and Williams, J. (2000), *Poverty and Social Exclusion in Britain* (York: Joseph Rowntree Foundation, York Publishing House).

Goulborne, H. (1999), 'The Transnational Character of Caribbean Kinship in Britain', in S. McRae (ed.) *Changing Britain: Families and Households in the 1990s* (Oxford: Oxford University Press).

Graham, S. (1998), 'The End of Geography or the Explosion of Place? Conceptualising Space, Place and Information Technology', *Progress in Human Geography* 22:2, 165–85.

Granovetter, M. (1983), 'The Strength of Weak Ties: a Network Theory Revisited', *Sociological Theory* 1, 203–33.

Green, E.A. and Canny, A. (2003), *Geographical Mobility, Family Impacts* (Cambridge: Joseph Rowntree Foundation, Policy Press).

Green, N. (2002), 'On the Move: Technology, Mobility, and the Mediation of Social Time and Space', *The Information Society* 18, 281–92.

Grieco, M. and Raje, F. (2004), 'Stranded Mobility and the Marginalisation of Low Income Communities: An Analysis of Public Service Failure in the British Public Transport Sector', paper presented at Urban Vulnerability and Network Failure Conference, University of Salford, 29–30 April 2004, http://www.geocities.com/transport_and_society/networkfailure.html, accessed 10 March 2006.

Gustafson, P. (2002), 'Tourism and Seasonal Retirement Migration', *Annals of Tourism Research* 29:4, 899–918.

Hagman, O. (2006), 'Morning Queues and Parking Problems: On the Broken Promise of the Automobile', *Mobilities* 1:1, 63–74.

Haldrup, M. and Larsen, J. (2003), 'The Family Gaze', *Tourist Studies* 3:1, 23–45.

——— (2006) 'Material Culture of Tourism', *Leisure Studies* 25:3, 275–289.

Hall, C.M. (2005), 'Reconsidering the Geography of Tourism and Contemporary Mobility', *Geographical Research* 43:2, 125–39.

——— and Williams, M. (2002), *Tourism and Migration: New Relationships between Production and Consumption* (Dordrecht: Kluwer).

Hamill, L. (2005), 'Introduction: Digital Revolution – Mobile Revolution', in L. Hamill and A. Lasen (eds) *Mobile World: Past, Present and Future* (London: Springer).

Hammerton, J. (2004), 'The Quest for Family and the Mobility of Modernity in Narratives of Postwar British Emigration', *Global Networks* 4:4, 271–84.

Hampton, K. and Wellman, B. (2001), 'Long Distance Community in the Network Society', *American Behavioral Scientist* 45:3, 476–95.

Hannam, K., Sheller, M. and Urry, J. (2006), 'Editorial: Mobilities, Immobilities and Moorings', *Mobilities* 1:1, 1–22.

Harvey, D. (1989), *The Condition of Postmodernity* (Oxford: Blackwell).

Heath, C., Knoblauch, H. and Luff, P. (2000), 'Technology and Social Interaction: The Emergence of "Workplace Studies"', *British Journal of Sociology* 51:2, 299–320.

Heelas, P., Woodhead, L., Seel, B., Tusting, K. and Szerszynski, B. (2005), *Spiritual Revolution: Why Religion Is Giving Way to Spirituality* (London: Blackwell).

Henderson, S. and Gilding, M. (2004), '"I've Never Clicked This Much with Anyone in My Life": Trust and Hyperpersonal Communication in Online Friendships', *New Media and Society* 6:4, 487–506.

Hiller, H. and Franz, T. (2004), 'New Ties, Old Ties and Lost Ties: the use of the Internet in Diaspora', *New Media and Society* 6:6, 731–52.

Holmes, M. (2004), 'An Equal Distance? Individualisation, Gender and Intimacy in Distance Relationships', *Sociological Review* 52:2, 180–200.

Høyer, K. and Ness, P. (2001), 'Conference Tourism: A Problem for the Environment, as Well as for Research', *Journal of Sustainable Tourism* 9, 451–70.

Hubert, P.J. and Potier, F. (2003), 'What is Known?', in K.W. Axhausen, J-L. Madre, J.W. Polak and P.H. Toint (eds) *Capturing Long Distance Travel* (Naldock: Research Science Press).

Hulme, M. and Truch, A. (2004), 'Exploring the Implications for Social Identity of the New Sociology of the Mobile Phone', paper presented at The Global and the Local in Mobile Communication: Places, Images, People, and Connections Conference, Budapest, 10–11 June.

Ioannides, D. and Ioannides, C.M. (2004), 'Jewish Past as a Foreign Country', in T. Coles and T. Dallen (eds) *Tourism, Diasporas and Space* (London: Routledge).

Ito, M., Okabe, D. and Matsuda, M. (eds) (2005), *Personal, Portable, Pedestrian. Mobile Phones in Japanese Life* (Cambridge, MA: MIT Press).

Jarvis, H. (2005), 'Moving to London Time: Household Co-ordination and the Infrastructure of Everyday Life', *Time & Society* 14:1, 133–54.

Johnston, L. (2001), '(Other) Bodies and Tourism Studies', *Annals of Tourism Research* 28:1, 180–201.

Jones, R., Oyung, R. and Pace, L. (2002), 'Meeting Virtually – Face-to-Face Meetings May Not Be a Requirement for Virtual Teams', *ITjournal, HP*, http://www.hp.com/execcomm/itjournal/second_qtr_02/article6b.html, accessed 15 December 2004.

Kang, S. and Page, S. (2000), 'Tourism, Migration and Emigration: Travel Patterns of Korean-New Zealanders in the 1990s', *Tourism Geographies* 2:1, 50–65.

Kaplan, C. (1996), *Questions of Travel* (Durham, NC: Duke University Press).

Katz, J. and Aakhus, M. (2002a), 'Introduction: Framing the Issues', in J. Katz and M. Aakhus (eds) *Perpetual Contact: Mobile Communication, Private Talk, Public Performance* (Cambridge: Cambridge University Press).

—— (eds) (2002b), *Perpetual Contact: Mobile Communication, Private Talk, Public Performance* (Cambridge: Cambridge University Press).

Kaufmann, V. (2003), *Re-thinking Mobility and Contemporary Sociology* (Aldershot: Ashgate).

Kaufmann, V., Manfred, M.M. and Joye, D. (2004), 'Motility: Mobility as Social Capital', *International Journal of Urban and Regional Research* 28, 745–56.

Kennedy, P. (2004), 'Making Global Society: Friendship in Networks among Transnational Professionals in the Building Design Industry', *Global Networks* 4:2, 157–79.

—— (2005), 'Joining, Constructing and Benefiting from the Global Workplace: Transnational Professionals in the Building-Design Industry', *Sociological Review* 53:1, 172–97.

Kenyon, S., Lyons, G., and Rafferty, J (2002), 'Transport and Social Exclusion: Investigating the Possibility of Promoting Inclusion through Virtual Mobility', *Journal of Transport Geography* 10:3, 207–19.

Kesselring, S. (2006), 'Pioneering Mobilities: New Patterns of Movement and Motility in a Mobile World', *Environment and Planning A* 38, 269–79.

Kibby, M. (2005), 'Email Forwardables: Folklore in the Age of the Internet', *New Media and Society* 7:6, 770–90.

Klein, O. (2004), 'Social Perception of Time, Distance and High-speed Transportation', *Time & Society* 13:2/3, 245–63.

Kyle, G. and Chick, G. (2004), 'Enduring Leisure Involvement: The Importance of Personal Relationships', *Leisure Studies* 23:3, 243–66.

Larsen, J. (2004), '(Dis)Connecting Tourism and Photography: Corporeal Travel and Imaginative Travel', *Journeys: International Journal of Travel and Travel Writing* 5:2, 19–42.

—— (2005), 'Families Seen Photographing: The Performativity of Tourist Photography', *Space and Culture* 8:4, 416–34.

—— (2006), 'Geographies of Tourist Photography: Choreographies and Performances', in J. Falkenheim and A. Jansson (eds) *The Spatial Turn in Media Studies* (Gothenburg: Nordicom).

——, Axhausen, K and Urry, J. (2006), 'Geographies of Social Networks: Meetings, Travel and Communications', *Mobilities* 1:2, 261–283.

——, Urry, J. and Axhausen, K. (2006), 'Social Networks and Future Mobilities', report for the Department for Transport, UK (Lancaster University, Department of Sociology), http://www.lancs.ac.uk/fss/sociology/cemore/cemorepublications. htm, accessed 20 April 2006.

—— (forthcoming), 'Networks and Tourism: Mobile Social Life', *Annals of Tourism Research.*

Lasch, C. (1980), *The Culture of Narcissism* (London: Sphere).

Lash, S. and Urry, J. (1994), *Economies of Signs and Space* (Sage: London).

Lassen, C. (2006), 'Aeromobility and Work', *Environment and Planning A* 38:2 301–12.

Laurier, E. (2004a), 'Busy Meeting Grounds: The Café, the Scene and the Business', paper presented at International Specialist Meeting on ICT, Everyday Life and Urban Change, Utrecht, http://web.geog.gla.ac.uk/~elaurier/cafesite/texts/ elaurier007.pdf, accessed 20 December 2004.

—— (2004b), 'Doing Office Work on the Motorway', *Theory, Culture & Society* 21:4/5, 261–77.

—— and Philo, C. (2003), 'The Region in the Boot: Mobilising Lone Subjects and Multiple Objects', *Environment and Planning D* 21, 85–106.

——, Whyte, A. and Buckner, K. (2001) 'An Ethnography of a Café', *Journal of Mundane Behaviour* 2(2), 195–232.

Lethbridge, N. (2002), *Attitudes to Travel* (London: ONS).

Letherby, G. and Reynolds, G. (2003), 'Making Connections: the Relationship between Train Travel and the Processes of Work and Leisure', *Sociological Research Online* 8:3, http://www.socresonline.org.uk/8/3/letherby.html, accessed 30 November 2004.

Licoppe, C. (2004), '"Connected Presence": The Emergence of a New Repertoire for Managing Social Relationships in a Changing Communication Technoscape', *Environment and Planning D* 22, 135–56.

—— and Smoreda, Z. (2005), 'Are Social Networks Technologically Embedded? How Networks Are Changing Today With Changes in Communication Technology', *Social Networks* 27, 317–35.

Limmer, R. (2004), *Job Mobility and Living Arrangements: Mobility and the Cosmopolitan Perspective*, Cosmobilities Network, http://www.mobilitypioneers. de/Dokumente/download/Statement-Limmer-frei.pdf, accessed 15 January 2005.

Ling, R. (2004), *The Mobile Connection: The Cell Phone's Impact on Society* (San Francisco: Morgan Kaufmann).

Ling, R. and Yttri, B. (1999), *Nobody Sits at Home and Waits for the Telephone to Ring: Micro and Hyper-coordination through the use of the Mobile Phone*, FoU Report, 30/99 (Telenor: Telenor Forskning of Utvikling).

—— (2002), 'Hyper-coordination via Mobile Phones in Norway', in J. Katz and M. Aakhus (eds) *Perpetual Contact: Mobile Communication, Private Talk, Public Performance* (Cambridge: Cambridge University Press).

Liu, J., Daily G.C., Ehrlich, P.R. and Luck, G.W. (2003), 'Effects of Household Dynamics on Resource Consumption and Biodiversity', *Nature* 421: 530–3.

Löchl, M., Schönfelder, S., Schlich, R., Buhl, T., Widmer, P. and Axhausen, K.W. (2005) *Stabilität des Verkehrsverhaltens*, final report, SVI 2001/514, Schriftenreihe, 1120 (Bern: Bundesamt für Strassen, UVEK).

Lodge, D. (1985), *Small World* (Harmondsworth: Penguin).

Lyons, G., Jain, J. and Holley, D. (2005), *The Use of Travel Time by Rail Passengers in Great Britain*, (Bristol: Centre for Transport and Society, University of the West of England).

—— and Urry, J. (2005), 'Travel Time Use in the Information Age', *Transport Research A* 39, 257–76.

McCabe, S. (2002), 'The Tourist Experience and Everyday Life', in G. Dann (ed.) *The Tourist as a Metaphor of the Social World* (Wallingford: CABI).

MacCannell, D. (1976), *The Tourist: A New Theory of the Leisure Class* (New York: Schocken Books).

McGlone, F., Park, A. and Roberts, C. (1999), 'Kinship and Friendship: Attitudes and Behaviour in Britain 1986–1995', in S. McRae (ed.) *Changing Britain: Families and Households in the 1990s* (Oxford: Oxford University Press).

Marcus, G. (1998), *Ethnography through Thick and Thin* (Princeton: Princeton University Press).

Mason, J. (1999), 'Living Away from Relatives: Kinship and Geographical Reasoning', in S. McRae (ed.) *Changing Britain: Families and Households in the 1990s* (Oxford: Oxford University Press).

—— (2004a), 'Managing Kinship over Long Distances: The Significance of "The Visit"', *Social Policy and Society* 3:4, 421–9.

—— (2004b), 'Personal Narratives, Relational Selves: Residential Histories in the Living and Telling', *Sociological Review* 52:2, 162–79.

Massey, D. (1994), *Space, Place and Gender* (Cambridge: Polity Press).

May, J. and Thrift, N. (eds) (2001), *Timespace: Geographies of Temporality* (London: Routledge).

Miller, D. and Slater, D. (2000), *The Internet* (Oxford: Berg).

Mokhtarian, L.P. (1990), 'A Typology of Relationships between Telecommunications and Transportation', *Transport Research A* 24:3, 231–42.

—— (2003), 'Telecommunications and Travel', *Journal of Industrial Ecology* 6:2, 43–57.

Molz, J. (2004), 'Destination World: Technology, Mobility and Global Belonging in Round-the-World Travel Websites', unpublished PhD thesis (Lancaster University: Department of Sociology).

—— (2006), 'Watch Us Wander: Mobile Surveillance and the Surveillance of Mobility', *Environment and Planning A* 38:2, 377–93.

Nandhakumar, J. (1999), 'Virtual Teams and Lost Proximity: Consequences on Trust Relationships', in P. Jackson (ed.) *Virtual Working: Social and Organisational Dynamics* (London: Routledge).

National Statistics (2004), *Travel Trends 2003: A Report on the International Passenger Survey* (Newport: National Statistics).

Oigenblick, L. and Kirschenbaum, A. (2002), 'Tourism and Immigration: Comparing Alternative Approaches', *Annals of Tourism Research* 29:4, 1086–110.

Oksman, V. and Turtiainen, J. (2004), 'Mobile Communication as a Social Stage', *New Media and Society* 6:3, 319–39.

O'Hara, M., Perry, M., Abigail, S., Barry, A. and Brown, T. (2002), 'Exploring the Relationship between Mobile Phone and Document Activity during Business Travel', in B. Brown, N. Green and R. Harper (eds) *Wireless World: Social and Interactional Aspects of the Mobile Age* (London: Springer).

O'Reilly, K. (2003), 'When is a Tourist? The Articulation of Tourism and Migration in Spain's Costa del Sol', *Tourist Studies* 3:3, 301–17.

Ó Riain, S. (2000), 'Net-Working for a Living: Irish Software Developers in the Global Workplace', in M. Burawoy, J.A. Blum, S. George, Z. Gille, T. Gowan, L. Haney, M. Klawiter, S.H. Lopez, S. Ó Riain and M. Thayer (eds) *Global Ethnography: Forces, Connections and Imaginations in a Postmodern World* (London: University of California Press).

Papastergiadis, N. (1999), *The Turbulence of Migration: Globalization, Deterritorialization and Hybridity* (Cambridge: Polity Press).

Perkins, H. and Thorns, D. (2001), 'Gazing or Performing? – Reflections on Urry's Tourist Gaze in the Context of Contemporary Experiences in the Antipodes', *International Sociology* 16:2, 185–204.

Plant, S. (2000), 'On the Mobile: The Effects of Mobile Telephones on Social and Individual Life', http://www.motorola.com/mot/doc/0/234_MotDoc.pdf, accessed 7 March 2005.

Plaut, O.P. (2004), 'Do Telecommunications make Transportation Obsolete?', in S. Graham (ed.) *The Cybercities Reader* (London: Routledge).

Pons, O.P. (2003), 'Tourist Dwelling, Bodies and Places', *Tourist Studies* 3:1, 47–66.

Pooley, C. and Turnbull, J. (2000a), 'Commuting, Transport and Urban Form: Manchester and Glasgow in the Mid-Twentieth Century', *Urban History* 27:3, 360–83.

—— (2000b), 'Modal Choice and Modal Change: the Journey to Work in Britain since 1890', *Journal of Transport Geography* 8, 11–24.

Pooley, C., Turnbull, J. and Adams, M. (2005), A Mobile Century?: Changes in Everyday Mobility in Britain in the Twentieth Century (Aldershot: Ashgate).

Pratt, A. (2002), 'Hot Jobs in Cool Places. The Material Cultures of New Media Product Spaces: The Case of South of the Market, San Francisco', *Information, Communication and Society* 5:1, 27–50.

Pred, A. (1977), 'The Choreography of Existence: Comments on Hagerstrand's Time Geography and its Usefulness', *Economic Geography* 53, 207–21.

Pribilsky, J. (2004), 'Aprendemos a Convivir: Conjugal Relations, Co-parenting, and Family Life among Ecuadorian Transnational Migrants in New York and the Ecuadorian Andes', *Global Networks* 4:3, 313–34.

Putnam, D.R. (2000), *Bowling Alone: The Collapse and Revival of American Community* (New York: Simon & Schuster).

Rheinholdt, R. (2002), *Smart Mobs: The Next Social Revolution* (New York: Perseus Books).

Riley, R., Baker, D. and Van Doren, C.S. (1998), 'Movie Induced Tourism', *Annals of Tourism Research* 25:4, 919–35.

Ritzer, G. (2001), *Explorations in the Sociology of Consumption – Fast Food, Credit Cards and Casinos* (London: Sage).

Rojek, C. (1997), 'Indexing, Dragging and the Social Construction of Tourist Sights', in C. Rojek and J. Urry (eds) *Touring Cultures: Transformations of Travel and Theory* (London: Routledge).

Romano, N. and Nunamaker, J. (2001), 'Meeting Analysis: Findings from Research and Practice', proceeding from 34th Hawaii International Conference on System Sciences, http://csdl2.computer.org/comp/proceedings/hicss/2001/0981/01/09811072.pdf, accessed 1 February 2005.

Roos, P.J. (2001), 'Postmodernity and Mobile Communications', ESA Helsinki Conference: New Technologies and New Visions, 31 August, http://www.valt.helsinki.fi/staff/jproos/mobilezation.htm, accessed 1 April 2005.

Ryan, L. (2004), 'Family Matters: (E)Migration, Familial Networks and Irish Women in Britain', *Sociological Review* 52:3, 351–64.

Salaff, J., Fong, E. and Siu-Ling, W. (1999), 'Using Social Networks to Exit Hong Kong', in B. Wellman (ed.) *Networks in the Global Village* (Colorado: Westview Press).

Schafer, A. and Victor, G.D. (2000), 'The Future Mobility of the World Population', *Transportation Research Part A* 34, 171–205.

Schlich, R., Simma, A. and Axhausen, K.W. (2003), *Determinanten des Freizeitverkehrs: Modellierung und Empirische Befunde*, final report for SVI 73/00. Arbeitsberichte Verkehrs- und Raumplanung, 190 (Zurich: IVT, ETH).

——, Schönfelder, S., Hanson, S. and Axhausen, W.K. (2004), 'The Structures of Leisure Travel: Temporal and Spatial Variability', *Transport Reviews* 24:4, 219–28.

Schönfelder, S. and Axhausen, K.W. (2003), 'Activity Spaces: Measures of Social Exclusion?' *Transport Policy* 10:4, 273–86.

—— (2004), 'Structure and Innovation of Human Activity Spaces', *Arbeitsberichte Verkehrs- und Raumplanung*, 258 (Zurich: IVT, ETH).

Schwartzman, B.H. (1989), *The Meeting: Gatherings in Organizations and Communities* (Amsterdam: Kluwer Academic/Plenum Publishers).

Scott, J. (2000), *Social Network Analysis* (London: Sage).

Seaton, V.A. and Palmer, C. (1997), 'VFR Tourism Behaviour: The First Years of the United Kingdom Tourism Survey', *Tourism Management* 18:6, 345–55.

Sennett, R. (1999), *The Corrosion of Character: Personal Consequences of Work in the New Capitalism* (New York: W.W. Norton & Co).

Sheller, M. and Urry, J. (2006), 'The New Mobilities Paradigm', *Environment and Planning A* 38:2, 207–26.

Shove, E. (2002), 'Rushing Around: Coordination, Mobility and Inequality', Lancaster: Department of Sociology, Lancaster University, http://www.comp.

lancs.ac.uk/sociology/papers/Shove-Rushing-Around.pdf(02/11), accessed 18 November 2004.

Simmel, G (1997), 'The Metropolis and Mental Life', in D. Frisby and M. Featherstone (eds) *Simmel on Culture* (London: Sage).

Simonsen, K. (2003), 'Urban Life between Mobility and Place', *Nordisk Samhällsgeografisk Tidsskrift* 36, 27–47.

Smart, C. and Shipman, B. (2004), 'Visions in Monochrome: Families, Marriage and the Individualization Thesis', *British Journal of Sociology* 55:4, 491–509.

Smith, V.L. (ed.) (1978), *Hosts and Guests: the Anthropology of Tourism* (Oxford: Blackwell).

Standage, T. (2004), 'Virtual Meetings – Being There', *The Economist* 5/13/04, http://www.ivci.com/international_videoconferencing_news_051304.html, accessed 15 January 2005.

Stephenson, H. (2002), 'Travelling to the Ancestral Homelands: the Aspiration and Experiences of a UK Caribbean Community', *Current Issues in Tourism* 5:5, 378–425.

Sutton, R.C. (2004), 'Celebrating Ourselves: the Family Reunion Rituals of African Caribbean Transnational Families', *Global Networks* 4:3, 243–58.

Symes, C. (1999), 'Chronicles of Labour: a Discourse Analysis of Diaries', *Time and Society* 8:2, 357–80.

Tarry, C. (2003), 'The Difficult Part is Yet to Come: Profit rather than Traffic Alone Remains the Key to Airline Prosperity', *Tourism and Hospitality Research* 5:1, 79–83.

Thrift, N. (2000), 'Performing Cultures in the New Economy', *Annals of the Association of American Geographers* 90:4, 674–92.

—— (2004), 'Intensities of Feeling: Towards a Spatial Politics of Affect', *Geografiska Annaler Series B* 86, 57–78.

Toiskallio, K. (2002), 'The Impersonal Flâneur: Navigation Styles of Social Agents in Urban Traffic', *Space and Culture* 5,169–84.

Tooke, N. and Baker, M. (1996), 'Seeing is Believing: The Effect of Film on Visitor Numbers to Screened Locations', *Tourism Management*, 17:2, 87–94.

Townsend, A. (2004), 'Mobile Communications in the 21st Century City', http://urban.blogs.com/research/Townsend-TheWirelessWorld-BookChapter.PDF, accessed 30 July 2005.

Tuan, Yi-Fu (1977), *Space and Place: The Perspective of Experience* (Minneapolis: University of Minnesota Press).

Tzanelli, R. (2004), 'Constructing the "Cinematic Tourist": The "Sign Industry" of the Lord of the Rings', *Tourist Studies* 4, 21–42.

UNDP (2004), *Human Development Report 2004* (New York: United Nations Development Programme, UN).

Urry, J. (1990/2002), *The Tourist Gaze* (London: Sage).

—— (1995), *Consuming Places* (London: Routledge).

—— (2000), *Sociology Beyond Society: Mobilities for the 21st Century* (London: Routledge).

—— (2002), 'Mobility and Proximity', *Sociology* 36:2, 255–74.

—— (2003), 'Social Networks, Travel and Talk', *British Journal of Sociology* 54:2, 155–75.

—— (2004a), 'Connections', *Environment and Planning D* 22, 27–37.

—— (2004b), 'Small Worlds and the New "Social Physics"', *Global Networks* 4:2, 109–30.

—— (2004c), 'The "System" of Automobility', *Theory, Culture & Society* 21:4/5, 25–39.

Van Wee, B., Rietveld, P. and Meurs, H. (2006), 'Is Average Daily Travel Time Expenditure Constant? In Search of Explanations for an Increase in Average Travel Time', *Journal of Transport Geography*, 14:2, 109–22.

Vaze, V.S., Schönfelder, S. and Axhausen, K.W. (2005), 'Continuous Space Representations of Human Activity Spaces', *Arbeitsbericht Verkehr- und Raumplanung*, 295 (Zurich: IVT, ETH).

Veijola, S. and Jokinnen, E. (1994), 'The Body in Tourist Studies', *Theory, Culture and Society* 6, 125–51.

Vigar, G. (2002), *The Politics of Mobility* (London: Spon).

Vilhelmson, B. and Thulin, E. (2001), 'Is Regular Work at Fixed Places Fading Away? The Development of ICT-based and Travel-based Modes of Work in Sweden', *Environment and Planning A* 33, 1015–29.

Vertovec, S. (2004), 'Cheap Calls: The Social Glue of Migrant Transnationalism', *Global Networks* 4, 219–24.

Walby, S. (1997), *Gender Transformations* (London: Routledge).

Wang, N. (1999), 'Rethinking Authenticity in Tourism Experience', *Annals of Tourism Research* 26, 349–70.

Warde. A. and Martens, L. (2000), *Eating Out: Social Differentiation, Consumption and Pleasure* (Cambridge: Cambridge University Press).

Watters, E. (2004), *Urban Tribes: Are Friends the New Family* (London: Bloomsbury).

Watts, D. (2003), *Six Degrees: The Science of a Connected Age* (London: William Heinemann).

Wearing, B. and Wearing, S. (1996), 'Refocusing the Tourist Experience: the "Flâneur" and the "Choraster"', *Leisure Studies* 15, 229–43.

Weber, E.J. (1976), *Peasants into Frenchmen: the Modernization of Rural France, 1870–1914* (Stanford: Stanford University Press).

Weber, K. and Chan, K. (2003), *Convention Tourism: International Research and Industry Perspectives* (London: Haworth Press).

Weber, M. (1948), *From Max Weber: Essays in Sociology* (London: Routledge and Kegan Paul).

Wellman, B. (2001), 'Physical Place and Cyberplace: The Rise of Personalised Networking', *International Journal of Urban and Regional Research* 25:2, 227–52.

—— (2002), 'Little Boxes, Glocalization, and Networked Individualism', in M. Tanabe, P. Van den Besselaar and T Ishida (eds) *Digital Cities II: Computational and Sociological Approaches* (Berlin: Springer).

—— and Haythornthwaite, C. (eds) (2002), *The Internet in Everyday Life* (London: Blackwell).

——, Hogan, B., Berg, K. Boase, J., Carrasco, A.J., Côté, R., Kayahara, J.T.L., Kennedy, M.L.T. and Tran, P. (2005), 'Connected Lives: The Project', in P. Purcell (ed.) *Networked Neighourhoods* (Berlin: Springer).

Weston, K. (1991), *Families We Choose: Lesbians, Gays, Kinship* (New York: Columbia University Press).

Williams, D. and Kaltenberg, B. (1999), 'Leisure Places and Modernity: the Use and Meaning of Recreational Cottages in Norway and the USA', in D. Crouch (ed.) *Leisure/Tourism Geographies: Practices and Geographical Knowledge* (London: Routledge).

Williams, M.A. and Hall, M.C. (2000), 'Tourism and Migration: New Relationships between Production and Consumption', *Tourism Geographies* 2:1, 5–27.

——, King, R., Warnes, A. and Patterson, G. (2000), 'Tourism and International Retirement Migration: New Forms of an Old Relationship in Southern Europe', *Tourism Geographies* 2:1, 28–49.

Wittel, A. (2001), 'Toward a Network Sociality', *Theory, Culture & Society* 18:6, 51–76.

Wolff, K. (1950), *The Sociology of George Simmel* (New York: The Free Press).

Young, M and Willmott, P. (1962), *Family and Kinship in East London* (Harmondsworth: Penguin).

Index